W9-BSN-140

SONGS SUNG RED, WHITE, AND BLUE

Also by Ace Collins

Stories Behind the Best-Loved Songs of Christmas
Turn Your Radio On: The Stories Behind Gospel
Music's All-Time Greatest Hits

SONGS SUNG RED, WHITE, AND BLUE

The Stories Behind
America's Best-Loved
Patriotic Songs

Ace Collins

HarperResource
An *Imprint* of HarperCollins*Publishers*

HarperCollins books may be purchased for educational, business, or sales promotional use. For information please write: Special Markets Department, HarperCollins Publishers, Inc., 10 East 53rd Street, New York, NY 10022.

FIRST EDITION

Designed by Mary Austin Speaker

Library of Congress Cataloging-in-Publication Data has been applied for.

ISBN 0-06-051304-7

03 04 05 06 07 WB/RRD 10 9 8 7 6 5 4 3 2 1

To all those who have served and fought under the

flag of the United States of America and to those

who have supported these men and women

CONTENTS

INTRODUCTION

Though most of the songs in this book are very well-known and much loved, I chose them more for their impact on America's history than their popularity. I think these songs reflect who we are, while also showing how we have both changed and remained the same as a people and a nation. They have not only reflected history, they have also made history. And because of this, the stories behind each of them help us to better understand and know not just those who wrote these songs but America itself.

There are songs in this book, such as "God Bless America" and "America the Beautiful," that almost everyone knows. There are songs of war and others written to celebrate peace. The stirring strains of the military service anthems can be found in these pages, as well as numbers that were born in times of depression, protest, or misunderstanding. There are songs from the left and the right, from black and white, from rich and poor, from the city and farms.

These songs were written by immigrants such as Irving Berlin and proud native sons like George M. Cohan. The words of modern country music superstar Merle Haggard can be found in this book. Patriot Francis Scott Key shares space here with registered communist Woody Guthrie. A female teacher Katherine Lee Bates taught her greatest lesson with her contribution, as did a Baptist preacher named Smith. Their lives and the reasons they wrote were unique, but in the end it all came back to a special moment when thoughts of America drove them to put what was on their minds into verse. In doing so they each changed the nation they called home.

In a very real sense, this book is a musical biography of the "home of the brave and the land of the free." It is a history lesson played out in note and verse. It is both a celebration and a prayer. In other words, these songs present the rich and diverse story that is the United States of America.

Ace Collins

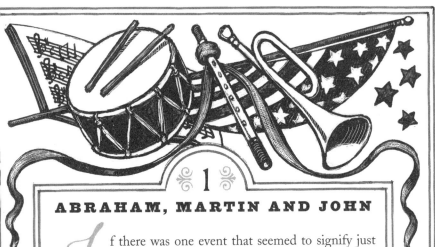

1

ABRAHAM, MARTIN AND JOHN

*I*f there was one event that seemed to signify just how tragic the Civil War had been, it was when the president was killed at Ford's Theatre. This action plunged a nation into deep despair and widened the gap between the victor and the loser. This death struck such a deep chord that in the months after Abraham Lincoln was assassinated by John Wilkes Booth, more than fifty songs were penned trying to capture the incredible sadness that had enveloped the war-scarred country. Yet while scores of these compositions were played in concert halls, churches, and theaters and around the fireplaces of common people, none managed to paint the graphic pain of the moment well enough to become a well-known American folk song or anthem.

It is doubtful that Dick Holler had ever heard any of the songs written about Lincoln's life and death. Yet in the wake of the assassination of another president, John F. Kennedy, Holler, like millions of other Americans, must have relived the details of the tragic deaths of both Lincoln and Kennedy. The parallels seemed uncanny, but in truth the deaths were most closely related by the fact that two men who seemed to have been the moral voices of the moment, men who were strongly loved and deeply hated for firing up incredible passions in their followers, had been struck down in what should have been the greatest moments of their lives.

Holler was not a historian, though he had a love of history. The man's claim to fame would come from writing about an American hero, though the star of his song was a hero of the fictional variety. In 1966, the rock group the Royal Guardsmen took Holler's "Snoopy vs. the Red Baron" to the top of the charts. This novelty number, inspired by Charles Schulz's classic comic-strip beagle, was equally enjoyed by old and young alike. If possible, it made Snoopy an even larger star than his bigheaded owner, Charlie Brown. Even as America laughed at his work and Holler deposited royalty checks from record sales, the man and the nation were still troubled by a host of problems plaguing the country—problems that a humorous song simply could not erase.

Much as Lincoln's death had scarred the United States for more than two decades, when Lee Harvey Oswald shot JFK, the wound festered in every facet of American society for years. Kennedy's loss left millions questioning every aspect of their lives, right down to the core of their beliefs. The death of the young president was even cited as a factor in the heated debates over integration and civil rights, the rapidly growing division between those who argued over the reasons for American involvement in Vietnam, and the accelerated experimentation with illegal drugs. Americans could not escape the bleakness of the times. The nightly news became a nightmare of disappointment and violence. Just when many felt that things could get no worse, another death brought the shocked nation to its knees again.

Dr. Martin Luther King Jr. was at the very least a controversial leader. As the man who jump-started the American civil rights movement, King was also a dynamic speaker whose ideas stirred up deep devotion, as well as deeply rooted fear. While millions of African Americans lined up to support his peaceful marches and demonstrations, the whites who clung to segregation saw him as the most dangerous man in the country. On a bright evening in Memphis, Tennessee, not long after making one of the most famous speeches of his life, King was gunned down on his hotel's balcony. It was April 4, 1968. King's death divided the nation much more deeply than had his life. In many parts of the country, violence erupted, and some areas began to take on the look of a war zone.

Like his older brother, the recently slain president, Robert Kennedy felt a calling to lead his nation. When Lyndon Johnson opted not to run for reelection in 1968, the younger Kennedy stepped in to try to win the role as the leader of the Democrats. When he won the California primary on June 4, 1968, he seemed well on his way to his party's nomination. After a rousing victory speech, he started to leave his hotel headquarters through the kitchen. Amid dirty dishes and late-night workers, the unthinkable happened when another assassin ended the life of the man millions called Bobby. A nation that had once felt so secure now shook and asked, "Who's next?"

In the wake of King's and the younger Kennedy's deaths, Americans began to wonder if every facet of a society that just a decade before had seemed so stable was now falling completely apart. Dick

Holler was one of those who were horrified. The songwriter sensed the national mood and saw a bridge that linked the deaths of three recent leaders to Lincoln's. That bridge was the mass of grief and questions that accompanied each death and the fact that the murders were fueled by each of the men's strong and courageous ideas and stands. With these thoughts fresh in his mind, Holler created a song that was uniquely American. It defied description—if the subject had not been so serious, this song might have been considered a novelty number. It wasn't a protest song, it wasn't an anthem, it wasn't a flag-waving ballad or a gospel standard, yet it contained elements of each of these styles. In just four verses and a chorus, it became much more than just another folk-pop standard.

What Holler's "Abraham, Martin and John" accomplished was to voice the pain and anguish of millions and ask the questions that haunted people all over the world. The song did not give answers, but rather pointed out that the ones who might have had those answers had been needlessly killed before they could share them with a needy nation. It was a song meant to stop the violence, but without a singer, it was also a song that only the writer knew. Without a special voice, the song's message would remain mute. So for America to hear this new song, Holler had to unite it with just the right artist. Ultimately, the person who would bring this new song to life was hardly known for singing anything with a deep message.

Dion DiMucci, known simply by his first name, had rocketed to fame with the group known as the Belmonts in the late 1950s. The New York City native and his three close friends rocked the charts with teenage love songs including "Where or When" and "Teenager in Love." Their sound was so good and their songs struck such a note with rock and rollers that the group quickly became royalty in the eyes of those who tuned in to watch *American Bandstand*. Many Belmont fans actually mourned when, in 1960, Dion left the group to try his luck as a solo act. The young man quickly scored two monster hits, "Runaround Sue" and "The Wanderer," and produced a number of other solid singles. Yet by 1964, as the British invasion put an end to the nation's fascination with teen idols and doo-wop music, Dion had all but dropped out of sight. He was searching for a way to break back onto playlists when he heard a demo of Holler's latest composition.

Though his teenage love songs had often led to Dion's being labeled a lightweight act, in truth he was a very spiritual man. He had probably scored so well with the teen audience in the early part of his career because he was perceptive enough to relate to their emotions. Now, at the age of thirty, he could relate just as well to the events that had so many Americans asking unanswerable questions. Holler's latest song was exactly the message Dion needed for his own life and what he felt America needed to hear as well. Though many doubted that the all but forgotten rock star, who hadn't hit the Top 40 in five years, could generate any airtime, Laurie Records, his original label, released the singer's simple and straightforward version of "Abraham, Martin and John." The executives at Laurie were probably just as shocked as anyone when the single shot up the charts. By November, just six months after the death of Bobby Kennedy, it had hit number 4, and it would ultimately be certified as a gold record. The song became a favorite with all ages and was cut by scores of other singers, including Marvin Gaye. Over the next two years it was sung in churches and at political rallies, peace demonstrations, and youth conferences. More than three decades after its release, millions can still recall enough of it to sing at least the chorus of "Abraham, Martin and John."

Though the singer would later reemerge as an important artist in contemporary Christian music, Dion would never again score another hit on the national playlists. Dick Holler would not hit the top of the charts another time either. Meanwhile, the United States and its people somehow worked through the turbulent sixties, dealt with the loss of three of the era's most influential voices, and moved on to a time when the generation gap would again narrow. Yet, thanks to Dick Holler's inspired words and Dion DiMucci's plaintive vocal, an introduction to three important men and their ideas were captured for posterity in the simple but moving song "Abraham, Martin and John." And today that most unusual of patriotic songs helps keep the spirit and the ideas of four very important Americans alive.

2

THE AIR FORCE SONG

he United States first developed a military flying corps in the days before World War I. Yet it was during that initial global war that pilots first began to gain a bit of prestige. After the conflict ended, the best minds in the military slowly began to realize that the airplane might play a much more significant role in future wars. Still, it took a bold move by Colonel Billy Mitchell, combined with the transatlantic flight of Charles Lindbergh, to finally convince most Americans that airplanes had a vital place in future military plans.

As the Army Air Corps grew, and more funding was set aside for this military department, its identity began to change. During the days when the nation was fighting the Great Depression, the Air Corps was developing into an almost separate branch of the service. It was obviously much different from any of the other army divisions in the simple fact that these men did not fight on the ground. In many eyes, the Air Corps made the rest of the army look as old-fashioned as horseback riders. So it was only natural that the cutting-edge men who flew the planes began to look for things, from hats to uniforms, that would distinguish them from other members of their service branch.

In 1937, Brigadier General H. H. Arnold, better known as "Hap," made an appointment with his commander, Major General Oscar Westover. As the chief of the Air Corps, Westover had more power than any other officer in the flying division of the army. "Hap" visited with his superior about the department's morale and recruiting more qualified men into the Air Corps in the future. Arnold felt that both of these problems could be diminished if the Air Corps had a higher individual profile. The general offered that a good place to start might be by securing their own song. He was convinced that an anthem could bring the group an identity that would set it apart from every other facet of the army. Besides, Arnold argued, there was a romance that went with the songs of the marines, the navy, and the army, and the Air Corps needed to exude that kind of aura as well. Westover readily agreed that a song might be a strong public-relations tool, but because he had no control over the Air Corps budget—the army staff decided where the money went—there were no funds to finance a new composition. Who would write for us for nothing? Westover wondered. When Arnold suggested a contest, Westover gave his approval, but only if "Hap" could find a donor for the prize. That is when a friend, Bernard MacFadden, stepped up to the plate.

MacFadden was the publisher of *Liberty* magazine. Along with *Colliers* and *Life,* at this time *Liberty* was one of the most read publications in the world. The periodical covered both news and personalities. In today's terms it was really a combination of *People, Time,* and *Entertainment Weekly.* Those who were famous and powerful read *Liberty* because they often found stories about themselves in the pages. Regular folks read *Liberty* to get the latest information and gossip on the famous and powerful, as well as news that might be of use in their lives. The rest of the magazine was filled with biographical features, reviews, and stories on everything from investment to health. The publication would cover anything that it deemed as news, and it spotlighted the sensational much more than the mundane. When Hollywood actress Jean Harlow died unexpected at the age of twenty-six in 1937, *Liberty* interviewed some of the best minds in the medical profession to find out how such a healthy young woman could have so quickly succumbed to kidney disease. With stories such as this, *Liberty* kept its readers on the edge of their seats, ready to rush out and grab the next issue as soon as it hit the newsstand.

MacFadden and the editors at *Liberty* were more than happy to offer a one-thousand-dollar prize to the winner of the Air Corps songwriter contest because it fit with the magazine's longtime approach to sales and exploitation—if you gave the reader a chance to win money, subscription and advertising sales would pick up. As one thousand dollars was much more than many Americans made in a year during the Great Depression, the head of *Liberty* was sure that hundreds of amateur songwriters would send in entries in an attempt to get the prize, and the newsstand sales of the magazine would shoot up, thus ensuring more sales of ads. To open up even more interest in the contest, the magazine could present a few features on the Air Corps and bring the readers up to date on what this branch of the army did. MacFadden felt that these kinds of features would keep the contest alive for months.

In its stories, *Liberty*, like many other publications, noted not only the variance in roles played by the Air Corps from other army divisions, but also the difference in the attitudes of those who were a part of this group. While these airmen had a military bearing, they seemed a bit more free spirited. Some even called them cocky. While their feet might rarely have been firmly planted on the ground, their actions in the sky certainly captured the imaginations of most of those who read the stories. These men were exciting daredevils who seemed to challenge death with every mission. There can be little doubt that the image created by *Liberty* and other magazines of the lone flier all but lost in the clouds certainly inspired many of the 650 contest entries.

Liberty's contest was geared for a two-year run. That seemed to be plenty of time to get several entries that would meet the Air Corps standards. But when a team of respected musicians, Mildred Yount, Hans Kindler, Rudolph Gands, and Walter Nash, gathered to make a final decision during the summer of 1939, the rosy picture suddenly grew dark. The quartet quickly realized that none of the contest songs was up to the task. So *Liberty* had to ask for even more submissions.

As the search for a song went forward, Westover was replaced with General Arnold as the Air Corps' head. Even though he had originally asked for a song, Arnold had no musical abilities. Realizing his limitations and tired of waiting on *Liberty*'s readers, Arnold asked famed composer Irving Berlin to write a song. Even the Master of Broadway could not come up with anything better than what more than six hundred amateurs had already submitted. By July, everyone was almost ready to give up and have the men of the Air Corps keep singing about the army's caissons.

On July 13, 1939, a private pilot, Robert Crawford, who also happened to be a pretty fair singer, approached Mildred Yount. Crawford was an Alaska native and a Princeton graduate, and had studied at the Juilliard School. He was also a well-known concert soloist. In truth, with his résumé, he probably should have been on the song committee. "The Flying Baritone," as he was called by *Time* magazine, sang Yount a number that he had dreamed up two days before. Yount was not just impressed, she immediately loved the new entry and slipped it in with a batch of the latest submissions for the committee to review. As Yount had figured, after almost two years of struggle, the frustrated board finally found something they liked. Crawford's song was a hit with the blue-ribbon panel and General Arnold.

Crawford would first perform the song at the Cleveland Air Races. He would sing "Off We Go" not just to the thousands gathered to watch the planes, but to a national radio audience as well. Then, on September 2, 1939, at a special banquet, he was given a check for one thousand dollars by *Liberty*'s MacFadden. As Crawford sang it again for the dinner guests, it finally seemed that the Air Corps had a song that was universally loved. Yet not everyone was impressed with Crawford's "Off We Go." Some very important forces stood opposed to this adoption.

Charles Lindbergh did not like the song at all. A host of other Air Corps vets also didn't think the number was regal enough for the flying corps. Some officers felt the song lacked grace and that the melody didn't soar like a modern plane. These groups of men argued for the search to go on. Yet their views were ignored because Crawford's song quickly became a favorite of most servicemen and civilians. General Arnold was such a fan of "Off We Go" that he posted the words and music inside uniform hats, in service manuals, on walls, and inside planes. He also had the Air Corps band play it at every gathering, large or small. But what fully established this anthem was the Second World War. As had been the original goal, the song even served to raise morale and interest in the Air Corps.

During World War II, "Off We Go" was used in several motion pictures, including the inspirational *Air Force* with John Garfield and Alan Hale. This movie, based on a real-life story, truly gave Crawford's song an international following and possibly did more for Air Corps recruiting than any other single influence during the war. Yet the song's writer was probably too busy flying planes for the Air Corps even to see the Warner Brothers' picture. Crawford was a pilot in the Air Transport Command throughout the war. Even after the fighting ended, he would remain in the reserves, where he gained the rank of lieutenant colonel. Today, Langley Air Force Base's Crawford Hall, home of the USAF Heritage of America Band, is named for the man who gave the air force its song.

The first page of the original score, the very paper that Crawford submitted to the selection committee in July 1939, was carried to the surface of the moon on July 30, 1971, aboard the *Apollo 15 Falcon* lunar module. The moment that the *Falcon* departed from the moon, a rendition of "The Air Force Song" was broadcast to the world by Major Alfred M. Worden, who was circling the moon in the command module. Robert Crawford had been dead for a decade and *Liberty* magazine had long ceased publication when the *Falcon* landed on the moon and "The Air Force Song" was played for the world. It seems a shame that the song's writer was not around to witness this event and the magazine was not there to record the moment when the "wild blue yonder" included more than just the earth and the sky, but all of outer space too.

3

AMERICA THE BEAUTIFUL

f all she had done was teach English, then Katherine Lee Bates would to this day be celebrated as one of the most gifted professors ever to set foot on the campus of Wellesley College. Her students loved her, and her ability to guide both her pupils and the institution's English department is still being felt more than seven decades after she died. Yet remarkably, Bates is not best remembered as a teacher, but as a patriot. This fiercely independent, heavyset New England matron gave her country one of its most beloved anthems. The fact that Bates was inspired to compose the lyrics to this song was a direct result of her thirst for knowledge, her desire to take part in new experiences, and her passion to share her adventures with others.

Bates did not have an easy childhood. Her father, a Congregational minister, died in the weeks after Katherine was born. Yet even in the worst of times, her mother and older brothers made sure that the baby of the Bates family received an education. In 1880, she accomplished the unthinkable: the young woman from a poor family worked her way through college and earned a degree from Wellesley.

Since childhood, Bates had felt a need to express herself in rhyme and verse. Beginning at the age of nine, she carried a notebook and pencil with her wherever she went. She was ready whenever inspiration struck. While still a college student, Bates had a poem, "Sleep," published in the prestigious *Atlantic Monthly*. A generation before, this same magazine had first published the work of another gifted American woman, Julia Ward Howe. Howe's "Battle Hymn of the Republic" would become the most important and inspiring anthem of the Civil War. Bates's "Sleep" did not immediately awaken the public's imagination as did Howe's "Battle Hymn," but the little poem did inspire the young woman to continue to write, and from that writing would come a song that would exceed even "Battle Hymn" in popularity and reach.

After teaching at a local high school for several years, Bates was asked to join the faculty at Wellesley. For the young woman it was a dream come true. Yet it was a different and temporary opportunity to instruct students that set in motion the events that would trigger the writing of "America the Beautiful."

In 1893, Bates was asked to journey west to teach a summer session at Colorado College in Colorado Springs. This was an adventure that the teacher could not turn down. Though she was still in the spring of her life, this would not be her first major tour. Two years before, she had spent a portion of her summer vacation in Europe. While she had loved the opportunity to see the grand history of the Continent, she was even more excited to see the rugged frontier of her own native land.

Bates's trip west took her through two major tourist destinations

O beautiful for spacious skies,
For amber waves of grain,
For purple mountain majesties
Above the fruited plain!
America! America!
God shed his grace on thee
And crown thy good with brother-
    hood
From sea to shining sea!

O beautiful for pilgrim feet
Whose stern impassioned stress
A thoroughfare of freedom beat
Across the wilderness!
America! America!
God mend thine every flaw,
Confirm thy soul in self-control,
Thy liberty in law!

O beautiful for heroes proved
In liberating strife.
Who more than self their country
    loved
And mercy more than life!
America! America!
May God thy gold refine
Till all success be nobleness
And every gain divine!

O beautiful for patriot dream
That sees beyond the years

Thine alabaster cities gleam
Undimmed by human tears!
America! America!
God shed his grace on thee
And crown thy good with brother-
    hood
From sea to shining sea!

ORIGINAL LYRICS
O beautiful for halcyon skies,
For amber waves of grain,
For purple mountain majesties
Above the enameled plain!
America! America!
God shed his grace on thee
Till souls wax fair as earth
    and air
And music-hearted sea!

O beautiful for pilgrims' feet,
Whose stern impassioned stress
A thoroughfare for freedom beat
Across the wilderness!
America! America!
God shed his grace on thee
Till paths be wrought through
    wilds of thought
By pilgrim foot and knee!

O beautiful for glory-tale
Of liberating strife

When once and twice,
   for man's avail
Men lavished precious life!
America! America!
God shed his grace on thee
Till selfish gain no longer
   stain
The banner of the free!

O beautiful for patriot dream
That sees beyond the years
Thine alabaster cities gleam
Undimmed by human tears!
America! America!
God shed his grace on thee
Till nobler men keep once again
Thy whiter jubilee!

and the nation's most fertile farmland. Each of these stops, as well as the views from her coach window, would set in place the foundation for a single dramatic moment of inspiration. The teacher took in the sights at Niagara Falls before boarding another train to Chicago. In the Windy City she attended the World's Columbian Exposition. This was essentially a world's fair celebrating Columbus's discovery of the New World. On display was the real Liberty Bell, as well as a new carnival ride called the Ferris wheel. At the exposition, "My Country 'Tis of Thee" was sung by a choir of ten thousand voices, and fireworks lit up the night skies. There could be little doubt that if Bates had stopped her trip at this point, she would have had a great deal to share with her friends and family and she would have seen more in a week than most Americans of her generation saw in a lifetime. Yet she pushed on west in order to teach English religious drama to students in the Rocky Mountains and view everything that was between Chicago and Colorado Springs.

At Colorado College, Bates gave herself fully to her classes, but her spare moments were spent touring the area. She saw everything she could see, often taking notes. On July 22, 1893, in the middle of her time in Colorado Springs, the teacher joined a tour group that was headed for the famed Pikes Peak. The trek up the 14,110-foot mountain took hours, but Bates didn't care. In her mind, every twist in the road held a new discovery. Finally, after seeing flowers, trees, mighty snowcapped peaks, and unimaginable drop-offs, the party arrived at the summit. There, surrounded by little more than thin air, the teacher looked to the east and saw the flat wheat fields that fed a nation. In the distance she also spotted cities and towns, rivers and roads, trains and tiny farmhouses. When she turned to the west, she observed a wall of mountains that were so high they seemed to touch the heavens. In those moments, the young woman was not just awed, but inspired. She would recall that the words of a poem came to her during these moments as if they had arrived on the wind.

"One day some of the other teachers and I decided to go on a trip to 14,000-foot Pikes Peak," Bates later wrote, explaining her inspiration on that July day. "We hired a prairie wagon. Near the top we had to leave the wagon and go the rest of the way on mules. I was very tired. But when I saw the view, I felt great joy. All the wonder of America seemed displayed there, with the sea-like expanse."

On that day Bates, as she so often did, picked up the notebook she always carried and jotted down each phrase that flew into her mind. Ultimately the most inspired verses of her life would also be the easiest to compose. Maybe that is why even the author did not at first realize the magnitude of what she had just written.

Bates did not rush out and share her new poem with the world. It would be several weeks later, in August, after she had gotten back to Wellesley, before she would even bother to read it again. When she did go back and study her words, she was apparently disappointed. Somehow, she inititially believed that these verses didn't measure up to what she had witnessed that day on Pikes Peak. In her own mind, no words, not even those in this poem, could soar as her heart did on that July afternoon.

After some polishing, Bates sent her "America the Beautiful" to the *Congregationalist*. This first published version of the poem appeared in that magazine on July 4, 1895. Within days a composer tried to match music to the teacher's lyrics. Silas Pratt was the first to write a melody for "America the Beautiful," but he would not be the last. More than seventy-five different tunes would be married to Bates's poem. Yet it would take a Baptist minister to find just the right tune to go with what was quickly becoming America's favorite patriotic ode.

Like many, Clarence A. Barbour felt that Bates's composition needed to be set to music. He pictured "America the Beautiful" as a hymn. In 1904, Barbour memorized the poem's words and meter, then began to go through songbooks trying to find an existing melody that matched Bates's work. The tune he finally uncovered was called "Marterna."

"Marterna" had been written by Samuel Ward in 1882. Unlike Bates, Ward was not inspired by the awesome beauty of nature; rather, it was a family trip to Coney Island that triggered his tune. The thirty-three-year-old church musician began to hum a new melody on a steamboat ride home from the park. He couldn't find paper to jot down the musical notes as they came to him, so he borrowed a friend's linen shirt cuff. Thus began the unique birth story of a tune that was destined to become the most familiar melody in America.

Ward matched his music to an old English hymn, "O Mother Dear, Jerusalem." This marriage of words and melody would first be published in 1888, in a monthly religious-music periodical, the *Parish Choir.* From there "O Mother Dear, Jerusalem" would find its way into several hymnals. As Ward listened to choirs sing his "Marterna," even he was awed by the beauty of the melody. Once he was brought to tears when a children's choir delicately moved up and down the scale with ease and grace while performing his composition.

Ward died a year before Barbour matched his music to Bates's poem, so the composer of "Marterna" never knew the full reach of his inspired work. First performed at the Lake Avenue Baptist Church in Boston, the newly merged lyrics and music quickly made their way into other churches, concert halls, and schools. In 1910, when Barbour placed this version of "America the Beautiful" into his best-selling *Fellowship Hymns,* the union seemed to be everlasting.

Katherine Bates gave up all royalties to her work when it was initially published. Likewise, Ward's family made no claim for payment when his melody was linked to Bates's poem. To Bates and the Ward family, this song belonged to the American people. It was their gift to a country that had allowed them to prosper doing what they so loved to do.

As Bates continued her writing and teaching, others in positions of leadership decided that "America the Beautiful" should be the official song of the land. Bills were introduced in Congress, hundreds of groups lobbied various presidents, and scores of editorials stated that "America the Beautiful" reflected the complete American story better than either of the other two unofficial national anthems, "My Country 'Tis of Thee" and "The Star-Spangled Banner." Yet in spite of the song's popularity, "America the Beautiful" would be a bridesmaid. On March 4, 1931, President Herbert Hoover signed a bill making "The Star-Spangled Banner" the nation's official song. For millions this seemed a travesty. Resolutions to overturn this choice and replace it with "America the Beautiful" would continue to surface for decades.

Bates kept busy writing and teaching to the end of her life, and died on March 28, 1929. She left behind many poems and stories that endeared themselves to millions. Yet it was her adventurous spirit that led to this poet creating a masterpiece that is still sung from sea to shining sea. It may not be the official national anthem, but more Americans probably know these words and can sing the simple tune to "America the Beautiful" than know and can sing "The Star-Spangled Banner." That fact would greatly please both Katherine Bates and Samuel Ward.

As a footnote, Katherine Bates didn't join the call to make her song the official anthem for the country. Perhaps she knew that "America the Beautiful" didn't need to be the anthem, because most Americans had already decided that it was the nation's national hymn.

Author's note: There has probably been more written about "America the Beautiful" than any song other than possibly "Silent Night." This chapter touches only the high points of this wonderful American hymn. To find out the complete story, please take the time to find and read Lynn Sherr's 2001 book, *America the Beautiful*. In this eloquently written work, the esteemed ABC-TV reporter presents a story that is as uplifting as the song. Ms. Sherr's research breaks new ground, and she wonderfully entertains as she informs. *America the Beautiful* is published by Public Affairs Books.

4

AN AMERICAN TRILOGY

ickey Newbury was born in Texas in 1940, and by the age of sixteen was singing rock and roll and had even landed a record contract. Yet he was not a typical rocker. In his spare time, when he wasn't on stage or at school, the teen read poetry from the pens of Keats and Wilde, and tried to put lyrics together in a thoughtful way. It was obvious to all who knew him that Mickey Newbury was a different kind of person, a boy whose introspective views of life were appreciated by only a few in a time when pop culture leaned more to drive-in movies about atomic monsters, hot rods, and going steady and when music embraced songs of teenage love and heartbreak.

After high school graduation and a few years working local clubs, Newbury joined the air force and left his Houston home for England. There he met Kris Kristofferson. Most thought the two young philosophers walked to a different beat and did not, in any shape or form, fit into the air force norm. They were right on both counts.

After being released from the service, Newbury landed in Nashville. He introduced his buddy Kristofferson to a friend in the publishing business, and soon, thanks to recordings by Johnny Cash and Janis Joplin, Kris was riding one of his own songs, "Me and Bobby McGee," to superstardom. Although Mickey wasn't being featured on national television shows or signing movie deals, he wasn't doing badly either. Newbury was penning hits for a host of Music City's finest and hanging out with the likes of Willie Nelson and Roger Miller. Yet by and large, the life that moved so seamlessly around Newbury was still not the same world that was reflected in his own thoughts.

By the late sixties, the uncomplicated post–World War II world had given way to the chaos of revolutionary times. The generation gap had grown to the point where it seemed no bridge could span the differences between young America and the establishment. The fight for equal rights for minorities had literally set cities ablaze and torn communities apart. The Vietnam War had further divided the United States; the flag and all that it had once stood for seemed forever lost. For the first time in a hundred years, the nation appeared ready to pull away into a dozen pieces. As millions looked for answers, Newbury's observations were suddenly relevant.

For a while, hits seemed to roll from Newbury's pen as easily as rain fell onto a tin roof. "Why You Been Gone So Long," "Sweet Memories," "She Even Woke Me Up to Say Goodbye," "How I Love Them Old Songs," and "Just Dropped In (To See What Condition My Condition Is In)" didn't just race up the charts; they all were recorded by more than a dozen different artists from every musical genre. Mickey penned number 1 records for Andy Williams, Eddy Arnold, Willie Nelson, Solomon Burke, and Kenny Rogers.

Newbury's work was so hot that his songs once topped four different charts—easy listening, R & B, country, and pop/rock—at the same time. To this day, no other singer or songwriter has ever accomplished that feat.

Newbury's status as a top Music City tune master put him on the road, where he worked some of the hippest clubs in the country. In the early seventies he was on the West Coast when the manager of the famous Bitter End issued a warning. This admonition set in motion a creative process that would bring three different elements from the Civil War together in a manner that helped bridge the current generation gap while offering a healing message to the entire nation.

"The manager told me that I couldn't sing the song 'Dixie,'" Newbury recalled. "He said his crowd would take offense at that kind of racist song."

The warning really came out of left field. The club manager must have thought that all Nashville acts paraded out the old battle standard whenever they played. At the time the songwriter had not even considered singing "Dixie." Yet while the song was not usually part of Newbury's show, the warning not to play it caused the young man to ponder why "Dixie" was off limits.

"I felt that 'Dixie' was not a racist song," Newbury explained. "It had been written by a man from New York. I didn't feel it was right that people had taken this old folk song and changed its meaning so that it was now considered inflammatory. So, in an attempt to change those views, I decided to sing the song, but in a different way, as a ballad."

Those who had come into the Bitter End were young and liberal, and were used to the messages found in Judy Collins and Joan

Baez songs. They were expecting nothing less antiestablishment from Newbury.

At a key moment during his set, with just his guitar and his voice, Mickey Newbury slowly and plaintively embraced each of "Dixie"'s words. As he did, a hush fell over the audience and people hung on every note, every phrase, and every verse. The rapt attention he had generated from the crowd did more than justify the singer's choice of the old song; it also set his mind to whirling.

"I don't know why," Newbury explained, "but I just moved naturally from 'Dixie' to 'The Battle Hymn of the Republic.'"

Unlike the choral versions that had been so identified with "Battle Hymn" over the years, Newbury's approach was simple and direct. It was more a prayer than a march, more a request than a demand. The audience, now almost entranced, considered the real message in the old song that had once spurred on Union troops in the Civil War and was now inspiring those who had latched onto the hope generated by Martin Luther King Jr. Now it wasn't about war; it was about truth.

The unusual concept of melding the old Southern anthem and the Northern battle song would have been novel enough on its own. Yet for reasons even he did not understand, the singer reached back into his memory and pulled out another song. It was one that he had listened to Harry Belafonte sing, a Negro slave spiritual from the West Indies about a dying man and his son.

"All My Trials" completed the story begun with "Dixie." Three songs that so defined the groups who had fought the Civil War were brought together in one place by one man. North and South, as well as black and white, were united. Though most in the audience that night didn't fully appreciate the message, and even Newbury didn't completely understand what he had just done, the war that had come to such a bitter end a century before and had caused such a great divide in America to that day had suddenly been presented that night, ironically at a place called the Bitter End, in a light that brought healing not anguish, love not hate, unity not division.

Because of the response Newbury received as he put "An American Trilogy" together on stage in Los Angeles, he cut the song. However, unlike the young audience at the Bitter End, America was not ready for this union of South and North, black and white. From both the left and the right, editorials were written and protests were filed against stations that played the song. Soon, as he became tired of being hounded by the press, even Newbury dropped it from his concert sets.

For reasons that are still unknown, one night a Memphis television station used "An American Trilogy" as its sign-off music. One of the few people still watching TV at that time of the early morning was Priscilla Presley. The wife of the King of Rock and Roll was deeply impressed with Newbury's arrangement of the three old American songs. Mrs. Presley took the song to her husband, and within a few weeks Elvis was singing "An American Trilogy" on stage.

"When Elvis sang it and recorded it," Newbury explained, "it saved the song. When he sang it, people understood the message. He was probably the only one in the world who could have made it work."

As much as any song Presley ever recorded, "An American Trilogy" became his theme song. It would be the last song he ever sang in public when he closed his final concert with it before he died. Thanks to Elvis, Newbury's inspirational arrangement began to inspire other vocalists from every facet of entertainment. Ninety-two artists, from Led Zeppelin to Enrique Chia, from the Osmonds to Randy Travis, from Tanzorchester Klaus Hallen to the London Symphony Orchestra, have recorded it. It has been performed around the world and has become the song that many believe defines the total American experience better than any other ever written.

Mickey Newbury could have heeded the words of a nightclub manager on that night so long ago. He could easily have been too scared to perform a song that might stir up feelings of hate and prejudice. But what the manager did not know and the audience could not see was that Newbury had that same kind of grit and courage that had inspired and motivated Americans to go against the grain for generations.

5

ANCHORS AWEIGH

*C*harles A. Zimmermann seemed destined to a life in the service. The son of a navy man, Zimmermann grew up listening to his father's stories about the Civil War. The elder Zimmermann had played in the Union's navy band during the war with the Confederate States and had been a part of famous battles that were still very much recent history. The navy vet was honored that he had answered the call, helped preserve the nation, and inspired the troops by playing songs such as "Hail Columbia," "Columbia the Gem of the Ocean," and "Rally Round the Flag." While Charles was proud of his father and the time he had courageously given to his country, it was his father's stories of music more than the talk of battle that seemed to pique the younger Zimmermann's interest. And it was this interest in music, combined with a sporting contest, that led the son's hand to create a musical identity for the navy his father so loved.

After high school, Charles attended and then graduated from the Peabody Conservatory in Baltimore, Maryland.

Even at a young age, he seemed to be a musician bent on composing. Perhaps he dreamed of a life in classical or popular music, but, if he did, those dreams ended in 1887, when the navy called. With very little thought and no apparent regrets, Zimmermann accepted the position as bandmaster of the Naval Academy Band. At the tender age of twenty-six, Zimmermann was barely older than the students in his band, and like them, he was energetic and always looking for a way to mix modern musical sounds with the traditional military march tunes. Though no one could have guessed it at the time, this was a marriage that would last until death.

Unlike any bandmaster who had come before, Zimmermann reshaped the music of the school and provided sounds that intrigued student and serviceman alike. He might not have been a genius, but he was hardworking and intent on delivering the same kind of inspiration leading the band as his father once had playing in it. He was as devoted to his position as any instructor in Annapolis.

Five years into his job, "Zimmy," as he was affectionately known by the midshipmen, gave the gift of a new march song to the graduating class of 1892. This vibrant composition became so popular and was so appreciated that the class presented the bandmaster with a gold medal at graduation. This honor spurred Zimmermann on, and for the next thirteen years he wrote a new march for each class, until he had no room left on his jacket for the gold medals.

By 1906, Lieutenant Zimmermann and his music were as much a part of the Naval Academy as uniforms, freshman hazing, and the American flag. In his two decades at Annapolis, he had become an institution, and so had his class march songs. Yet before the musician could begin to compose a march tune for the class of '07, he was approached by Midshipman First Class Alfred Hart Miles. Miles wanted to change dramatically the tenor of Zimmermann's next piece. He wanted the new song to serve not as inspiration in the classroom or on the battlefield, but rather as a rallying cry for the gridiron. Little did either of them guess that the student's suggestion would lead to a song that would become as well known as almost any other tune in American history.

During Zimmermann's tenure at the academy, football had become the major focus on campus. The game had grown from a school intramural novelty into warfare on the grass. Football had evolved to the extent that it was the measuring stick as to who was bigger, mightier, and tougher, the army or the navy. The games between West Point and the Naval Academy had become more than simple grudge matches: the pride of each branch of the service demanded victory each year. Thousands of alumni and all the students turned out for each contest. Their cheers could be heard for miles. The fans of the team who won partied all night; the losers mourned as if they had just lost their best friend.

In every football game that had been played during his years as a student, a disheartened Miles had watched as Army had beaten Navy. As another of the annual sporting wars drew near, the student decided that something had to be done to end the cavalry's reign and return bragging rights to those who ruled the seas. With this in mind, he felt a need to invent a catalyst that could fire up the Blue. Miles felt the answer to his challenge could best be found in a new musical number. So he suggested that Zimmy put some bounce and energy into his next class march and, by doing so, compose a fight song that could make its debut at the upcoming Army-Navy gridiron clash. As the student later put it, "We were eager to have a piece of music that would be inspiring, one with a swing to it so it could be used as a football marching song." Little did he know that the song he helped create would move out of a football stadium, circle the globe, and become the single tune that sent millions of U.S. sailors off to battle for the next century.

Navy legend has it that after discussing the student's ideas for a new class song, Zimmermann and Miles went to the Naval Academy Chapel and sat down at the organ. The bandmaster played around with some original tunes until he came up with something the student liked. On that cool November day, as Zimmy fleshed out the melody, Miles first wrote the two verses of a march the men entitled "Anchors Aweigh." This original song was filled with digs at Army, support for the Navy squad, and a host of football-inspired phrases. A few weeks later the composition was played by the midshipmen band and sung by the brigade at the Army-Navy football contest. It was an immediate hit, and as Miles had hoped, his beloved Navy team finally won. Scores embraced this new song as the academy's rabbit's foot.

It is not known if the bandmaster attempted to create any other marches that year. If he did, he evidently did not find one that surpassed the football march. So Zimmermann presented "Anchors Aweigh" to the class of 1907 as their song. Yet while other Zimmy pieces had left the campus when each class did, to be forgotten by the new students that followed, this song didn't leave the Naval Academy. The next year it was played and sung at every football game. Within a few years, "Anchors Aweigh" had so grown in stature at Annapolis that it was even adopted by the United States Navy as the official song of the seafaring branch of the service.

For almost two decades, a period that included "Anchors Aweigh" being played and sung all over the world during the First

World War, the song remained just as Zimmermann and Miles had penned it. But by 1926 times had changed, and Midshipman Royal Lovell felt a need to update the old fight standard to better reflect its status as the song of the entire U.S. Navy.

Zimmermann's tune and arrangement remained just as they had been written at the organ in November 1906. Lovell felt that certain lyrical elements could also be kept and were important to the song's message. As the sailor's "weigh" came from the archaic word meaning to heave, hoist, or raise, and "aweigh" signified that this action had been completed, the title would be unchanged. After all, even a modern navy had anchors that had to be pulled from the bottom. And this event was and is still duly noted in every ship's log. Yet other original fight-song phrases just did not work for the navy at sea. After all, during a time of war, the army was not the enemy. Lovell examined each line and reworked them as needed.

Lowell retooled the verses to reflect the mission of every navy man, whether he had been to the academy or not. He also deleted a reference to celebrating and drinking after a win (a line that had been removed by the academy several years before but was still being sung by many alumni). With this reworking, "Anchors Aweigh" truly did become a song that would stand the test of time, an anthem for every day, not just for that one day a year when Navy and Army met on a football field.

Alfred Miles left Annapolis to became a career navy officer. He would retire as a captain, but his hand in writing the service branch's official song would mean that his touch would never leave the navy he so loved. Lowell's impact would remain after he left the service as well.

Charles Zimmermann, who had begun the tradition that was

really responsible for inspiring the musical effort, would continue to write class songs, though none would ever find the fame of "Anchors Aweigh." He would also continue to be an inspiration, a friend, and an icon at the school. In 1916, those who composed the *Lucky Bag,* the academy yearbook, decided it was time to honor the bandmaster. On the very first page of the annual, the students created a layout that featured Zimmy in his full-dress uniform. The entire next page was filled with words of tribute to the man and his devotion to the United States Naval Academy. The students could hardly wait to present Lieutenant Zimmermann with the first copy of that year's *Lucky Bag.* Sadly, they never had the chance to properly unveil their surprise.

Zimmermann suddenly became ill on Sunday morning, January 16, 1916. Within hours a brain hemorrhage had drained the life from the body of the man who had become a campus institution. He was only fifty-four years old. Annapolis and the entire navy were left in shock. Hundreds of his former students came back three days later when Zimmy was given a full military funeral with midshipmen serving as pallbearers. His remains still rest on campus.

It was a shame that the honor that the academy had intended for Zimmermann was not revealed during his life. Yet the man with the baton did live long enough to realize the ultimate honor that any military bandmaster could ever know: to see and hear his own composition become the anthem for his branch of the service and also become one of the most recognized musical pieces in the entire world. Zimmermann also had the satisfaction of knowing that his song was given credit for ending Army's long string of football victories. To this Naval Academy man, that might even have been the most important honor of all!

6

THE ARMY SONG

*D*uring the early years of the twentieth century, the Philippines was not a duty tour that many soldiers requested. In the days before air travel, this island nation was a very long way from home. Yet thanks to a victorious outcome in the Spanish-American War, the Philippines, along with Puerto Rico and the Virgin Islands, had fallen under the American umbrella, so bases had to be built and maintained on these islands. In order to defend our new possessions, men like Edmund Gruber had to board troopships to go to these bases, many that didn't appear on most maps. Though it was not extremely dangerous duty, even though Filipino rebels were occasionally picking fights, it was still a difficult transition for most men.

Lieutenant Gruber arrived in the Philippines in 1908. A member of the field artillery unit, the officer found the islands both beautiful and haunting. There were breathtaking visions of natural glory all around the young man, but there were also constant cultural reminders that this place was much different from the United States.

Much of the Philippines is made up of rugged country. It was a tremendous undertaking to take the horse-drawn artillery wagons and cannons up and down the mountains and valleys that surrounded Gruber's camp. The few roads that existed were poorly maintained. For Gruber, his men, and the horses and mules, moving about the country was a task that often seemed to be impossible. Yet, because they were in the United States Army, they had to do the impossible at least once a week.

The rigors of training, watching his men push through unforgiving jungles and mountains, battling both harsh elements and native diseases, inspired Gruber to look for a way to ease the burdens of his hardworking unit. He noted that the long-held army tradition of singing songs during marches seemed to make the day pass more quickly. To give his men something new and more personal to sing, the officer penned a poem about their duties and set the verses to a folk-type tune. As the officer had hoped, it was an immediate hit with those stationed in the Philippines. The new song did indeed stoke morale and bring a new energy to daily chores. Soon "The Caissons Go Rolling Along" was not being sung just by Gruber's men; it had crossed the Pacific, brought back by soldiers returning from Philippine tours of duty, and was picked up by army personnel stationed in the United States. When he returned to the States and discovered that thousands knew his song, the officer was amazed.

A decade later, during the First World War, John Philip Sousa decided that Gruber's song needed to be updated and refined. The legendary bandleader rewrote the music into a march. He also renamed "Caissons." Though the words remained the same, it was now known as the "The Field Artillery Song." Sousa would take the reworked number to all of America through live performances, recordings, and sheet music. By 1930, "The Field Artillery Song" had become one of the most familiar and used songs in Sousa's pet project, music education in the public schools.

When Gruber wrote the song, almost everyone, including civilians, knew what the lyrics meant. Yet, as motor vehicles took over the tasks performed by mules and horses, the lyrics' meaning began to become a mystery. Though millions of schoolchildren would sing the song almost daily, by 1940, few knew that a caisson was an ammunition wagon, that a dale was a valley, and that "calling off your numbers" was a literal roll call of the various artillery batteries. Yet even though much of the meaning had been lost, "Caissons" was such a fun song to sing that it remained a favorite with young and old alike.

During World War II, American soldiers brought "The Field Artillery Song" around the world. They not only sang it as they marched, but they taught it to children at every stop along the way to Berlin and Tokyo. By the time the war had ended, millions who could not speak a word of English could sing every word of the army's unofficial song.

In 1956, when a future army man, Elvis Presley, was introducing a new kind of music to the world, Dr. Harold W. Arberg decided to touch up the song that Gruber had written and Sousa had rewritten. He especially wanted to change the lyrics so that they had a timeless meaning and real substance. When Arberg finished, he handed his work over to military brass in Washington. They were so impressed with "The Army Goes Rolling Along" that on December 12, 1957, this new version of the traditional number was designated the official song of the United States Army. For millions this announcement came as a great shock. Most believed that "Caissons" had been the official army song for decades. What would shock them even more was that the new version of "Caissons" no longer even mentioned the caissons!

In an attempt to introduce Arberg's new words and arrangement to a wider audience, the U.S. Army Chorus, backed by the U.S. Army Band, released a recording of "The Army Goes Rolling Along" in 1958. It did not receive a great deal of airplay, but the record did put a final stamp on the song that had come to define this branch of the military service.

Though much of what Edmund Gruber first penned has been changed, the message really remains intact. In 1908, Gruber's men had to work against great odds to be ready to roll in the Philippines. Today, though the challenges and equipment are much different, the United States Army must continue to be constantly ready to protect freedom and ensure liberty. So while the duties and job of the army have changed and become even more challenging, Gruber's song still defines the way that the army "keeps rolling along."

7

THE BALLAD OF
THE GREEN BERETS

*I*n 1961, just months into his presidency, John F. Kennedy took an interest in the army's elite Special Forces Corps. Kennedy, who as a naval officer in World War II had lived out some very heroic moments behind enemy lines in the Pacific, was convinced that men who volunteered for risky duty and special missions deserved to be singled out in some unique way. The army brass disagreed with the president. In the minds of those who officed at the Pentagon, a simple patch on a uniform sleeve was all the identification the men of the Special Forces needed. The army's top officers argued that an important facet of military discipline was to place no group apart from another group except by marks of earned rank. Kennedy, who had seen other nations' Special Forces detachments set apart in several ways, overruled those at the Pentagon. He ordered that the men serving in the elite Special Forces unit of the United States Army should be issued green berets as a "badge of recognition" for their skills, training, and courage. Yet four years later, even as that unique headgear appeared on battlefields in Southeast Asia, the American public had little idea what a Green Beret really was.

Author Robin Moore's best-selling book *The Green Berets* awakened a portion of the United States to the existence of the elite squad. The book would eventually become a forgettable movie starring John Wayne. But while the book and movie might have established an identity for the battle group, they did not make it a military icon. Without the input of a high school dropout whose musical dreams had seemingly been dashed when he joined the service, the Green Berets would probably have remained one of the army's least-known units.

Barry Allen Sadler was born in Carlsbad, New Mexico, on November 1, 1940. Thus began a life that was tragically short and by and large unhappy. Sadler's parents divorced not long after his birth, and his mother took her two sons on a gypsylike ride that would not end for Barry until the boy quit school and joined the air force at seventeen. Between his parents' divorce and the time Barry enlisted, he lived in Ruidoso, Hobbs, Santa Fe, Las Vegas, El Paso, Midland, Lubbock, Phoenix, Tucson, Los Angeles, San Francisco, Denver, Leadville, and a half dozen other towns. Needless to say, his education and social skills suffered because of the family's constant movement.

After his basic training, the air force made an obviously bright Sadler a radar specialist, a job he did well but did not particularly like. When his tour of duty ended, the now twenty-one-year-old Barry happily walked away from the service and back into a civilian life he was ill-prepared to handle. He had few marketable job skills and no sense of direction, so things did not go well. With a wanderlust probably born in a youth spent on the move, Sadler lived the next two years traveling throughout the West Coast doing odd jobs and singing in tiny nightclubs and bars. This life left the young man largely disillusioned, and broke. At a dead end, Sadler decided to go back to the only stable life he had ever known, the military.

Realizing that the air force would put him back in front of a radar screen, Sadler joined the army, where he went to airborne school. As he learned to jump out of planes, he became interested in the Special Forces groups that were training at Fort Bragg. Knowing the odds against completing the training were long, he nevertheless gave it a try. In the process, the young man went through almost a year of rigorous education that included demolition, karate, judo, communications, weapons, and intelligence. Sadler was one of the most dedicated soldiers in his group, and because of his discipline and effort, he would become one of only sixteen of his original class of fifty to graduate. Being presented with his own green beret was one of the proudest moments of his life.

Much like the Rangers of World War II and Korea, the Green Berets were dropped behind battle lines, where they would sabotage enemy movements and gather intelligence. Working in teams of a dozen men, they often stayed in hostile territory for months at a time, training locals to fight the enemy. Thus, they were not just soldiers; they were also teachers and ambassadors.

In Vietnam, Sadler, who had trained as a medic, often found himself not only in the thick of the action, but reaching out and helping civilians who had been caught between the two opposing sides. He compassionately doctored the injured even as he viciously fought the enemy. In the midst of a confusing and unpopular war, Staff Sergeant Sadler thrived as a soldier until he was injured by a booby trap. When an infection almost cost him his leg, the twenty-five-year-old man was sent back to a hospital in the States. Though this transfer deeply disappointed Sadler, it set in motion an improbable series of events that would make him a household name, the living icon for Army Special Forces, and for a while one of the most divisive symbols in the country.

In the mid-sixties Vietnam had become a political nightmare for the Johnson White House and the entire military. Millions were protesting American involvement in the war, and scores of politicians and entertainment stars were leading movements to end U.S. fighting in the region. Whereas a few years before, the military had been lionized in books, on television, and in motion pictures, it was now being demonized in print, in song, and on screen. Rather than being celebrated for their sacrifice and service to their country, men like Sadler were often reviled and singled out as what was wrong with America. The country had not been this divided since the Civil War. Some predicted that the United States would suffer a revolution. Others believed that the nation's glory days were behind it.

As he recovered in the army hospital and went through rehab, the good-looking Sadler was approached and asked if he would like to make fifty dollars as a model. This strange job offer came about thanks to best-selling author Robin Moore's book on Vietnam.

In 1963, Robert Kennedy, who had attended Harvard with Moore, pulled the strings necessary to allow the author to go with the Green Berets on missions in Vietnam. Moore actually had to complete the same training as had Sadler to make the trip. After several months in the rice paddies of Southeast Asia, Moore returned home and penned his book *The Green Berets*.

To lend a feeling of authenticity, Moore wanted to use a real member of the Special Forces unit on the cover. On a visit to Green Beret headquarters, Sadler caught the writer's eye. Thus, it was a uniformed Barry who posed for the cover of Moore's *The Green Berets*. During the photo session, Sadler also charmed the book's writer with his stories and wit. After the young soldier completed his work, he returned to his room and pulled out a song that he had begun even before he had been shipped out to Vietnam.

Sadler would later tell a reporter, "I began to think about writing a song involving the airborne when I earned my silver wings. I had no idea what it would be, but I wanted it to include the line, silver wings upon their chests." That line in a song that remained unfinished for two years would help to make Sadler the poster boy for a troubled military.

As he finished an elementary three-chord melody and matched it to the poem he had written about his own Special Forces group, an idea took root. Within weeks Sadler had convinced his commanding officer to take his songs to some of the local military brass. Needing some positive PR, the army decided to use the sergeant's material to pump up falling morale.

Initially the army brought Sadler into a studio and recorded a cheap version of some of his compositions for military use only. Yet when Robin Moore, whose book had just been released, received a copy of the material from Sadler, the author saw a larger audience for the project. He believed that one of the songs could make an impact on regular playlists as well. Moore also knew that if Sadler's ballad could find its way onto the national charts, it would be good for his book as well. The writer got a tape to Nashville record executives in the late fall of 1965. Upon hearing the rather crude and ragged recording, the largest studio on Music Row bit.

On December 18, 1965, backed by an orchestra made up of some of the finest musicians in Music City, Staff Sergeant Barry Sadler recorded a complete album in little more than twelve hours. The first song from that effort, "The Ballad of the Green Berets," was released a month later. Though shipped to both country and rock stations, RCA figured that if the song had a chance, it would be with the conservative crowd who listened to and bought country music. In this case, the experts were dead wrong.

"The Ballad of the Green Berets" should not have been able to strike the passionate chord it did in 1966. Yet in the midst of the folk rock era and anti–Vietnam War protests, Sadler sang what millions of Americans who had lived through World War II wanted to hear—a patriotic ode that saluted the brave men who fought and died in Vietnam "for those oppressed" by what many saw as an evil regime.

"The Ballad of the Green Berets" took off like a shot, selling faster than any RCA release in history. Two million copies were shipped in the first five weeks of release. After less than six weeks on the charts, "The Ballad of the Green Berets" knocked Nancy Sinatra's "These Boots Are Made for Walkin'" out of the top spot on *Billboard* magazine's rock playlists. It would hold that position for a month. On the country side, the single climbed to the number 2 position. In the process of watching his hit climb to the top, Sadler became the poster boy for the all-American hero and the Special Forces. He was featured in *Life, Time, Newsweek, Variety, Billboard,* and *Cash Box* magazines. The army also gave him an extended leave so that he could sing in uniform on *The Ed Sullivan Show, The Jimmy Dean Show,* and *The Hollywood Palace.* Sadler would receive a gold record for both his initial single and his album. Though Moore's book had to be helped by the exposure and sales of "The Ballad of the Green Berets," the song was by far a bigger hit and made a much deeper impression.

For a short time, "The Ballad of the Green Berets" had a strong impact on the politics and spirit of the nation. It temporarily blunted the antiwar sentiment and helped military recruiting. With millions memorizing the song and singing along with it on the radio, soldiers were again looked upon as men of honor. Kids even played G.I. Joe games in their yards. Yet, though the song he wrote remained a popular military march number and helped put the Special Forces into the spotlight, neither Sadler nor his hit could long turn the tide against a mounting national mood to end the war in the faraway Asian jungle. The song also did not pave the way to a better future for its writer.

Barry Sadler had been a solid member of the Green Berets and a good soldier. But while this affiliation made him a national icon for the Special Forces, it also became an albatross around his neck. Even after he left the service, few saw him as anything but a military man—a very unpopular image at the time—and no one accepted him as a serious musician. In the entertainment world he was thought of as nothing more than a one-hit phenomenon. Though he would write more songs and find some success with a series of novels, he never again regained the national spotlight. And until he tragically died in 1989, the result of a still-unexplained gunshot wound, Sadler would remain linked to Vietnam and all its bad memories.

A generation has come and gone since the Vietnam War. In the aftermath of the terrorist acts of 2001 in New York and Washington, those who serve in the military are again revered with pride, distinction, and honor. In actual combat, books, and movies, the Special

Forces have finally earned the recognition that John Kennedy demanded they receive. "The Ballad of the Green Berets" brings Americans together to honor those who have chosen to serve as members of the most elite forces of the military.

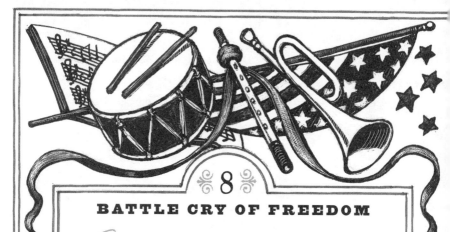

❧ 8 ❧

BATTLE CRY OF FREEDOM

eorge Frederick Root was born outside Sheffield, Massachusetts, on August 30, 1820. One of eight children, Root grew up when America was still a struggling nation unsure of its place in the world. He would live through the country's expansion west, a gold rush, a war that all but tore the nation in two, and the beginning of an industrial revolution that would make the United States one of the greatest nations in the world. Root not only witnessed a great deal of this firsthand, but he would set an important part of America's history to music.

As the new democracy felt its way along, the boy George Root lived in a world filled with farmwork and music, as well as tales of the Revolutionary War and the War of 1812. Though his family was of German descent (their original name had been Wurzel, German for "root"), once they landed in the United States, the Roots were patriots who celebrated all things American. Thus, besides the hymns and folk songs that were sung by most New Englanders, the Root family often gathered around the piano and sang such patriotic numbers as "Bunker Hill" and "John Jones."

One of George Root's five sisters, Francis, was a piano teacher and vocal instructor. Her thirst to learn everything she could about music was shared by George. They often sang and performed together in church, at local community gatherings, and in the family home. These performances would prove to be the foundation on which the young man would build the remainder of his life.

In 1838, Root left home and moved to Boston. There the teenager took piano lessons and, to help pay his bills, also played the organ at Winter Street and Park Street Churches. He expanded his education by taking voice lessons and by joining the Handel and Haydn Society. After two years of study, he became an instructor at Lowell Mason's public school, and a year later he was teaching voice lessons on his own.

In 1844, Root moved to New York City and began training voices at Abbott's School for Young Ladies. One of his first students was a blind girl named Fanny Crosby. Crosby, who would become one of America's greatest hymn writers, composing scores of standards such as "To God Be the Glory" and "He Hideth My Soul," was deeply influenced by her teacher. In part because of Root's work with Crosby, the woman would reshape religious music for the next century.

In 1845, Root married the prominent Mary Olive Woodman. Five years later the couple and their growing family moved to Paris, where Root studied classical voice with some of Europe's greatest teachers. When he returned to the United States in 1853, he joined with Lowell Mason in establishing the Normal Musical Institute. One of those hired by Root as an instructor was William Bradbury,

NORTHERN VERSION

Yes, we'll rally round the flag, boys,
   We'll rally once again,
Shouting the battle cry of Freedom,
   We will rally from the hillside,
We'll gather from the plain,
   Shouting the battle cry of
     Freedom.

Chorus:
The Union forever,
   Hurrah! boys, hurrah!
Down with the traitors,
   Up with the stars;
While we rally round the flag, boys,
   Rally once again,
Shouting the battle cry of Freedom.

We are springing to the call
   Of our brothers gone before,
Shouting the battle cry of Freedom;
And we'll fill our vacant ranks with
   A million free men more,
Shouting the battle cry of Freedom.

We will welcome to our numbers
   The loyal, true and brave,
Shouting the battle cry of Freedom;
And although they may be poor,
   Not a man shall be a slave,
Shouting the battle cry of Freedom.

So we're springing to the call
   From the East and from the
     West,
Shouting the battle cry of Freedom;
And we'll hurl the rebel crew
   From the land that we love
     best,
Shouting the battle cry of Freedom.

SOUTHERN VERSION

Our flag is proudly floating
   On the land and on the main,
Shout, shout the battle cry of
     Freedom!
   Beneath it oft we've conquered,
And we'll conquer oft again!
   Shout, shout the battle cry of
     Freedom!

Chorus:
Our Dixie forever!
   She's never at a loss!
Down with the eagle
   And up with the cross!
We'll rally 'round the bonny flag,
   We'll rally once again,
Shout, shout the battle cry of
     Freedom!

Our gallant boys have marched
   To the rolling of the drums,

Shout, shout the battle cry of
    Freedom!
    And the leaders in charge cry
    out,
"Come, boys, come!"
Shout, shout the battle cry of
    Freedom!

They have laid down their lives
    On the bloody battle field,
Shout, shout the battle cry of
    Freedom!
    Their motto is resistance—

"To tyrants we'll not yield!"
Shout, shout the battle cry of
    Freedom!

While our boys have responded
    And to the fields have gone,
Shout, shout the battle cry of
    Freedom!
Our noble women also
    Have aided them at home,
Shout, shout the battle cry of
    Freedom!

who would later write the music for "Jesus Loves Me," "Sweet Hour of Prayer," and scores of other well-known hymns.

Continuing to branch out, Root became a partner in the Chicago-based music publishing firm of Root and Cady. This educational-oriented company sold instruments and songbooks to schools and music societies, as well as publishing a magazine, the *Song Messenger of the Northwest*. By the late 1850s, Root was well known and respected by almost everyone in concert and educational-music circles as a teacher, arranger, administrator, and publisher.

Carving out a reputation as one of America's best classical music teachers and publishers put the real George Root in between a rock and a hard place. While he loved classical music, he also reveled in the parlor songs of his youth. Behind closed doors he would play and sing such songs as "Yankee Doodle," "Greensleeves," "Home Sweet Home," and "Pop! Goes the Weasel." He would also thrill his children by writing his own folk songs and singing them beside the fireplace at night. Because he had a reputation to maintain in classical circles, for several years he kept his folk songs to himself. When he finally did decide to publish them, he made sure that no one would know that he had written the little ditties.

In 1853, a previously unknown composer named G. Friedrich Wurzel wrote a song that would sweep across pubs and homes throughout America. "The Hazel Dell," a bright little folk song, was a major hit. Two years later Wurzel followed with "Rosalie the Prairie Flower." Like his initial offering, it was also a best-seller in sheet-music sales. With other songs like "There's Music in the Air," "Flee As a Bird," and "The Vacant Chair," Wurzel quickly became established as one of America's hottest songwriters. Yet when newspapers and magazines tried to find the writer and interview him, no one knew where he lived. One of those most unable to help the reporters was George Root.

Root's secret life as Wurzel would probably have gone to his grave if not for Lincoln's election and the secession of the Southern states from the Union. The Civil War that resulted from these actions suddenly created a call for folk music that could inspire a nation on the brink of destruction. Now the songwriter was no longer afraid to reveal his other personality; his country called and he responded.

Lincoln might have led the government and Grant the army, but it was Root who would lead the spirits of all Americans with music. Root, no longer using the pseudonym Wurzel, gave himself freely to the task of composing music that reflected his own feelings about his country and the war. His songs "We Shall Meet but We Shall Miss Him," "Just Before the Battle, Mother," and "Tramp! Tramp! Tramp!" were sung by soldier and civilian alike. The classical music authority quickly became recognized as the most popular tunesmith in America. Though he would compose more than a hundred songs during the war and eventually pen more than a thousand pieces of music before he died in 1895, most of what he wrote has been forgotten today. Yet there is one Root song that has survived and still remains one of the greatest patriotic standards ever written.

Root was both inspired and hurt by the division that the Civil War created in America. He had problems fathoming how friends and families could be so divided that they would gladly meet on battlefields to kill each other. He had close friends who now considered him an enemy. He knew men who had once been in the U.S. military who now spit on the very banner under which they had once proudly served. The pain and anguish he felt when he considered these events, and the anger and sadness that consumed him when he read of the tens of thousands of dead and wounded, made the writer more determined to tell the story of an America that was of one mind, body, and spirit. Like Francis Scott Key, Root believed that nothing so signified the glory of the Union as did the flag.

For Root the process of delivering a song of pride that captured his emotions would not be an easy endeavor. He knew the melody had to be simple and the words had to be straightforward and easy to remember while also trumpeting the cause of freedom. There could be no classical facets to this number; it had to be a people's song in order to trumpet a people's cause.

Root delivered a song that openly and boldly stated his beliefs that slavery was morally wrong and that any man who fought against the Union was a traitor. It was a masterpiece that combined both a march song and folk song feel. Because he was living in Chicago, the songwriter turned to two of the nation's most famous singers, Jules and Frank Lubard. The brothers were performing in the Windy City the night after Root had finished his latest composition. The crowd gave the new song a standing ovation and demanded an encore.

A week later the Hutchinson Family, a musical ensemble, premiered "Battle Cry" in New York in front of a huge political rally at Union Square. The response was the same.

"Rally Round the Flag" was an immediate hit in Chicago and New York. Within weeks of its publication, the song was being sung in churches and schools, at concert halls, and even by the men in blue as they marched off to battle. Many of the time credited the song, now commonly known as "The Battle Cry of Freedom," with being one of the best recruiting tools of the Civil War. Over the years, the song grew to mean so much to the Union cause that it turned the tide of real battles. On May 6, 1864, soldiers of the Ninth Army Corps were literally running for their lives from a Confederate assault. As they retreated, a voice was heard above the cannon fire, gunshots, and screams. One man boldly singing "The Battle Cry of Freedom" brought order to the chaos. The Union troops regrouped, turned around, and charged the enemy. As they fought to a decisive victory, they sang in unison Root's anthem.

Yet as Root proudly watched the North adopt his newest work, someone in the South rewrote his blatantly pro-Union composition and turned it into a Confederate battle song. "Our Dixie Forever" became just as big a hit below the Mason-Dixon line as did "Rally

Round the Flag" in the North. While this might have upset Root, it also showed how timeless and inspired was his melody.

Root's side won the war, and his original lyrics were retained, as was his reputation as one of America's greatest folk song composers. Though few today know its name, almost everyone knows the melody to "The Battle Cry of Freedom." This standard has sent American soldiers off to war countless times since it was written in 1862. It has been used in movies, on television programs, and by concert bands on thousands of occasions, and everyone from the Army Choir to the Andrews Sisters has sung it in America and on battlefields around the world. Of the hundreds of songs written especially for the Civil War, only "The Battle Hymn of the Republic" is better known or more beloved.

For the rest of his life, Root would stand out as a writer of popular music. His reputation as a composer of popular music outshone his work in classical music.

9

BATTLE HYMN
OF THE REPUBLIC

attle Hymn of the Republic" is America's most deeply spiritual anthem. Even as a majority of this nation's politicians attempt to keep a strong line between church and state, this old song blurs that line in every phrase and verse. At state dinners, Independence Day celebrations, and government-sponsored concerts, the obvious Christian theme of the "Battle Hymn" is overlooked in much the same way as the equally straightforward message of "Amazing Grace." For reasons that few understand, both of these songs evoke a patriotic pride that transcends the fact that they are really hymns. And in the case of "Battle Hymn," rather than a verse of Scripture or a life-altering event, the inspiration for this classic was a war that threatened the very core of this nation.

On a warm night in 1861, Julia Ward Howe was riding in a horse-drawn coach through the nation's capital with her husband, Dr. Howe; a minister friend, Dr. Clarke; and Governor Andrews of Massachusetts. The scene around them was chaotic. Thousands of Union troops were marching in every street, preparing for a looming battle with soldiers from the thirteen slave states that had broken off and formed a new confederation. Abraham Lincoln was an unproven leader, and millions were asking if the impending battles were worth the price the country would have to pay just to preserve the Union. With men shouting, cursing, and shooting guns in the air, the lone woman in the coach wondered if the whole world was going mad.

As the party slowly made its way through the streets, Dr. Clarke noted a group of men gathered outside an inn singing "John Brown's body lies amouldering in the grave." Rather than inspiring the minister's patriotic spirit, the image of seeing drunken men singing about a once proud man now rotting in the soil disgusted him. He glanced toward the Howes and declared that a tune so robust should not be coupled with words so dismal. Those around Clarke nodded in agreement.

After an hour on the unruly streets, the Howes returned to their hotel room, where they spent the remainder of the evening discussing the state of the Union. They questioned whether the drunken men that they witnessed falling out of taverns could possibly save the country. They also wondered how many of these men would be dead by this time next year.

It was a depressed Julia Howe who brushed her hair that night. As she looked at her own image in the mirror, she saw the horrors of war. Although she was exhausted, she was unable to think of anything but pain and suffering. She was also unable to rid her mind of the morbid song she had heard on the carriage ride. Even after she had turned down the lamp and gone to bed, the thoughts of death

Mine eyes have seen the glory of
   the coming of the Lord;
He is trampling out the vintage
   where the grapes of wrath are
   stored;
He has loosed the fateful lightning
   of his terrible swift sword:
His day is marching on!

Chorus:
Glory, Glory, Hallelujah! Glory,
   Glory, Hallelujah!
Glory, Glory, Hallelujah! His
   truth is marching on!

I have seen him in the watchfires of
   a hundred circling camps;
He hath builded him an altar in the
   evening dews and damps;
I have read his righteous sentence
   by the dim and flaring lamps:
His day is marching on!

Chorus

I have a read a fiery gospel; writ in
   burnished rows of steel

"As you deal with my comtemners,
   so with you my grace shall deal";
let the hero born of woman, crush
   the serpent with his heel:
Since God is marching on!

Chorus

He has sounded forth the trumpet
   that shall never call retreat;
He is sifting out the hearts of men
   before his judgement seat;
Oh be swift my soul to answer
   him! Be jubilant, my feet:
Our God is marching on!

Chorus

In the beauty of the lilies Christ
   was born across the sea,
With a glory in his bosom that
   transfigures you and me;
As he died to make men holy let us
   die to make men free:
While God is marching on!

Chorus

and destruction and the images of young men shooting each other on smoke-filled fields raced through her mind.

As her husband slept beside her, Howe began to quietly sing "John Brown's Body." At first she mouthed the words she had heard that afternoon, but soon, new lyrics leaped into her mind. They were words that seemed both to fit her grave mood and to sum up the solemn task that her nation faced. Buoyed by this inspiration, she picked up pen and paper and attempted to compose a poem set to the cadence of "John Brown's Body." As Mrs. Howe was a very religious woman, it was hardly surprising that the words she set on paper reflected not only the conflict at hand, but her own faith.

Mine eyes have seen the glory of the coming of the Lord;
He is trampling out the vineyards where the grapes of wrath are
stored;
He has loosed the faithful lightning of his terrible swift sword:
His truth is marching on.

Julia stayed up all night working on the verses to her "Battle Hymn." At daybreak, she woke her husband and sang the finished song to him. Deeply moved, Dr. Howe encouraged her to polish it. Over the next few days, Howe did much to refine the song that had been inspired by both hopelessness and hope, fear and strength.

A week later, when she had returned to her home in Boston, Julia shared "Mine Eyes Have Seen the Glory" with close friend James T. Fields. Fields was the respected editor of one of America's most popular publications, the *Atlantic Monthly*. He was touched by the message he found in Howe's work. Even more important, Fields thought "Battle Hymn" suited the spiritual needs of a nation deeply divided. In early 1862, the *Atlantic Monthly* brought Julia's song to the United States public. The response of those in the North was overwhelming. It was reprinted in numerous magazines and newspapers. President Lincoln voiced his love for the new "Battle Hymn," and government forces adopted it as their theme song.

As Confederate soldiers began to hear the strains of "Battle Hymn" from across the lines, many wondered about the irony of matching Howe's lyrics with the the tune to "John Brown's Body." The melody had actually been taken from a southern folk song, and the original lyrics spoke of the wonderful life that existed in the states now fighting to leave the Union. Of course, the rallying cry for the Rebels, "Dixie," had actually been written by a New Yorker who had never been across the Mason-Dixon line, so there was great irony hidden in the two songs that rallied both sides during this horrible war.

"Battle Hymn of the Republic" was a song of the moment and a commentary for the times. It had been written for the war that Julia Howe so feared and despised. The lyrics, though rich in religious imagery, really embraced the sights and sounds of the conflict between the states. Thus, it should have quickly faded into oblivion, like most other Civil War camp songs. Yet it did not. Instead it was embraced by African Americans as a symbol of what the war had given them. In black America, "Battle Hymn" was considered an anthem of freedom, promise, and hope. So while scores of other Civil War songs waned, in churches and celebrations freed slaves and their offspring kept Howe's work in the public eye.

In 1911, a daughter was born to a stevedore in New Orleans. It would be this woman who would take "Battle Hymn of the Republic" to the masses and make it a song beloved by all those who embraced American ideals.

Mahalia Jackson was singing in her church choir before she could read. By the time she was ten, her voice could bend the blues like the legendary Bessie Smith's. Yet Jackson didn't really care much for the blues—they were too sad. She wanted to sing happy songs that made people feel good.

Migrating to Chicago in her teens, Mahalia worked as a maid until she met up with gospel songwriter and choir director Thomas A. Dorsey. Dorsey seemed convinced that Mahalia's voice came straight from heaven, and therefore no one had the right to tamper with it. Not wanting to change her unique style and phrasing, Dorsey didn't allow her to sing with his world-famous choir, take voice lessons, or work with other writers. He demanded only that the young woman just "sing it the way she felt it."

During the depression, Jackson quickly rose to the ranks of the best-known female African American singers in the nation. Fronting for Dorsey's choirs, she cut records, appeared on radio, and brought the house down at the Apollo Theater. By 1950, she had toured Europe and sung for presidents and kings. To many, both white and black, she was the essence of African American music. With her deliberate, carefully paced, dramatic renderings of songs such as "Move On Up a Little Higher," "Keep Me Every Day," and "America the Beautiful," she thrilled millions. Often imitated, she was never equaled.

Those who accompanied Jackson were awed not only by her voice, but also by her presence. She never apologized for being a woman or being black. She had such a strong personality that even men who professed racist feelings bowed before her. She was also a woman of action who felt her voice had to stand for more than just quickly forgotten lyrics.

A child of the South, Mahalia Jackson boldly took her place in the forefront of the battle for civil rights. A hundred years after Julia Ward Howe wrote the words to "Battle Hymn of the Republic," Mahalia sang the song in front of hundreds of thousands at civil rights rallies, in churches, and at banquets and concerts. Through her voice and power she transformed the old southern folk song and the inspired lyrics of a cultured Bostonian into one of the most powerful patriotic anthems in history. She blended North and South, black and white, rich and poor, and made the song a part of the very fabric of America. When she sang it, freedom really did ring!

The most wonderful thing about the way Mahalia performed "Battle Hymn" was that she never moved the piece along at the same pace. As she sang she allowed a spirit to guide her emotions, her inflections, and her speed. Embracing each word to fully emphasize its meaning, she brought new light to the song each time she sang it. One could hear her sing Howe's song a hundred times and never hear it the same way twice. For that reason, she held her audiences spellbound, thus allowing every audience to glory in the song's message. She also made the number timeless, inspired hundreds of new choral arrangements, and defined it not as a "Battle Hymn," but an anthem of promise, freedom, and hope for all those who called America home.

It now seems appropriate that a southern-born black woman singer took the words that once rallied troops fighting for her ancestors' freedom and transformed those lyrics into a testament of hope for all people of all races. Mahalia Jackson's music was built on the faith of both white and black, was American in every way, and she blended it into a voice of universal belief in a color-blind God and a color-blind nation. Howe might have written the song, yet it was Mahalia who really defined what it has come to mean to all Americans.

10

THE BATTLE OF NEW ORLEANS

he Battle of New Orleans" is not played at Independence Day parades or military homecomings. This song is not a staple of the Marine Corps Band or a part of any official government ceremony. "The Battle of New Orleans" is usually found on the playlists of oldie radio stations, and it is not one of the tunes used during these stations' salutes to America's patriotic holidays. Yet this unique song, the product of an Arkansas schoolteacher's fertile imagination, needs to be included in any book about American patriotic music. "The Battle of New Orleans" stands apart from all other songs because of the unique story behind its inspiration, and the fact that it celebrates an important moment in American history that should never have happened.

James Morris grew up in the Ozark Mountains playing music and writing poetry. "Driftwood," Morris's nickname since birth, was proud to be a member of a family that included several generations of "hillbilly" singers. Not only did the Morris clan compose much of what they performed, but most of their instruments were homemade. Radio, easy transportation, and good roads might have opened up the country to all Americans, but they also began to take away the nation's distinct regional identities. So during the Great Depression, the Morris family represented a lifestyle and a craft that were quickly disappearing. By the time World War II moved the United States into the center of the world's stage, there were few places left where folk music traditions existed in their purest form.

Up until World War II, most hillbillies stayed pretty close to home from birth to death. Most boys usually followed in their father's footsteps as storekeepers, blacksmiths, or farmers. Yet the few young men who did leave to seek work in the cities, rarely came home. Jimmy Morris broke both of those molds.

Upon high school graduation, the young man traveled to Conway, Arkansas, where he studied at Arkansas State Teachers College (now the University of Central Arkansas). When he obtained a degree, Driftwood had his first chance to explore the country. With his education, this bright and creative man could now get a job that paid a great deal more money in one year than his parents had probably made in a lifetime. Yet, in the midst of the Great Depression, the country boy returned to his roots to teach the children of family friends. By 1936, Mr. Morris, as he was called by his students, was an underpaid and overworked twenty-nine-year-old Snowball, Arkansas, schoolteacher. Like almost all educators, he had discovered that most of his charges didn't care at all about what he was trying to teach. As much as they did not like math, spelling, and reading, Morris's sixth-grade pupils hated history more. Using every method he had learned in school and read about in teachers' training manuals, the man tried to tell the nation's story. Each day he was greeted by more and more yawns and uninterested looks.

Maybe much more for Morris than other teachers of the day, getting kids motivated to learn seemed important. Unlike a generation before, if these Arkansas kids dropped out of school without a diploma, there was very little that they could do. With the industrial age in full swing, unskilled jobs were growing harder and harder to find. Once, no one had asked the question "Do you have a high school degree?" but now it was the way most job interviews began. Morris also knew that even a high school diploma would not take these children very far up the economic ladder. To really make it in the world of tomorrow, the very same world that these children would live in as adults, it would take a college degree.

One night, after he had graded a batch of papers and prepared another day's lesson plans, Driftwood picked up his homemade guitar. As he plucked the strings, he considered the history lesson he was scheduled to try to teach the next day. As he played an old square dance tune called the "The Eighth of January," he began to visualize the events that were a part of the War of 1812. This was a colorful era, it was a time filled with drama, suspense, and heroism. Washington, D.C., had been burned by the British, the United States had been invaded by thousands of enemy soldiers, and everything that had been gained in the Revolutionary War was almost lost. The teacher then thought, if Hollywood would turn this story into a movie, then his kids could easily learn the facts they needed to know. A moment later, inspiration struck.

Morris picked up pencil and paper and began to jot down the high points of his next lesson. After writing a quick outline, he reconstructed his phrases into a long, rambling poem. As he had just played "The Eighth of January," his writing took on that song's meter and phrasing. A few minutes later, the teacher was singing an exciting and somewhat exaggerated version of the day the Americans whipped the British at the Mississippi River's end.

It was this history, set to a poem's rhythm, that finally captured his students' interest. As they listened to Morris's often colorful lyrics, they quickly learned about the important events and people that figured in this battle that happened days after the War of 1812 had actually ended.

"The Battle of New Orleans" quickly became a class favorite. Morris then set more historical events to music, and the Snowball sixth graders soon were as fascinated by history as was their teacher.

For the next twenty years, Morris took his musical teaching aids with him wherever he taught. While it did bring him great satisfaction, it did not bring Morris any financial rewards. It was pretty commonly known that in the 1950s few folks were any poorer than Arkansas schoolteachers.

As Morris was concluding his second decade as an educator, a Missouri hillbilly who had dropped out of school long before eighth grade became a star on Red Foley's *Ozark Jubilee* television show in Springfield, Missouri. He might have been undereducated, but the savvy Porter Wagoner knew that he needed to find some solid songwriters to provide him with hit records. As most of the well-known songwriters were already penning hits for more established acts, Porter decided to send his friend and publishing partner, Don Warden, on a trip through the Ozarks to uncover unknown song scribes.

In 1957, Warden heard about a songwriting schoolteacher who

lived in the tiny town of Timboe. Warden wrote down Jimmy "Driftwood" Morris's name in an old notebook and hit the road to find him. He struck out. There was no Driftwood or Morris listed in the Timboe telephone book. Little did Warden realize that at the time the teacher didn't even have the money for a telephone.

Warden reported what he had heard about Morris to Wagoner. Porter, who had just landed a spot on Nashville's *Grand Ole Opry*, encouraged his friend to keep looking. With nothing to lose but the cost of a stamp, Warden wrote the teacher in care of the Timboe post office. A few weeks later he received an answer. Morris acknowledged in his reply that he had written a few songs and that if the publisher wanted to come by, he would play them for him.

Warden didn't want to drive a couple of hundred miles on hilly, unpaved roads to hear an unproved talent, so he wrote back and asked Morris to put some of his songs on tape. The teacher replied that he would love to do that, but no one in Timboe had a tape recorder. The teacher then suggested that the men meet in Nashville during a school holiday. Morris had always wanted to spend some time in Music City and this seemed like a great way to take a vacation and maybe make some money too.

Warden and Morris first got together in a cheap hotel room. Over the course of an hour, the teacher played a wide variety of his tunes, numbers that ran the gambit from love songs to folk music. The publisher was not impressed with any of what he heard. As Warden got up to leave, Morris began playing "The Battle of New Orleans." Warden immediately sat back down. After Morris had finished, the publisher grinned and asked the teacher to play that song again. The next day Warden introduced Morris to RCA's top man in

Music City, Chet Atkins. It only took one listen to "New Orleans" to persuade Atkins to sign the educator to a record contract.

In his first recording session, RCA had the teacher cut a dozen songs. The label then released an album with high hopes of carving out a niche for the singing teacher in folk music. RCA and Atkins pumped Jimmy Driftwood, as they called him, to radio stations and the media. But no one bit. Only WSM radio in Nashville would play "The Battle of New Orleans," and because the lyrics contained the words "damn" and "hell," the station that was home to *The Grand Ole Opry* would spin the single only in the middle of the night. Knowing math as well as history, Morris headed back to Arkansas, realizing that he was better off teaching than trying to make money in the music world.

Like Morris, Johnny Horton was a country boy who loved to write music. He also once dreamed of teaching. He had attended Baylor University, where he had made the basketball team, but Horton couldn't shake his love of music long enough to finish his geology degree. Leaving college, he formed a band and began to tour. By 1958, the singer had a recording contract with Columbia, was a regular on the *Louisiana Hayride,* and had a fairly strong regional following in the South, but to make the move to the national spotlight, he needed a hit. One dark early morning, Horton was driving back from a late-night, small-town concert gig listening to WSM when he heard "The Battle of New Orleans." He immediately loved the historical ode and felt he had finally found the vehicle that could take him to the big time.

While Horton was sold on "New Orleans," Columbia was not. Folk music simply didn't sell, so the label suggested that the singer look elsewhere for his next single. Horton would not give up and finally convinced Columbia to at least let him record Morris's song. His arrangement of "The Battle of New Orleans" was so spirited and unique that the singer even managed to get his label to ship the single to radio stations. Still, no one in Nashville believed that this song about a little-remembered historical event would gain any real play time. So the Music City powers were stunned by the public's reaction to Horton's new single.

Just as it had done in that first Snowball, Arkansas, sixth-grade class, "The Battle of New Orleans" caused an immediate sensation. In a matter of weeks, Horton's record would climb to the top of both the country and rock music charts. This onetime teaching aid would become the biggest song of 1959 and one of the twenty-five top songs of the first five years of the rock and roll era. "The Battle of New Orleans" would make Johnny Horton a national sensation, pave the way for a resurgence of folk music, and spawn a historical-music craze that brought the nation scores of hits, including "Johnny Reb" and "Sink the Bismarck." This song also made Jimmy Morris one of the wealthiest teachers in the Ozarks.

Johnny Horton would hit number 1 on the country charts one more time with "North to Alaska" before dying in an East Texas car wreck. Though his voice was silenced at a very young age, his music is still being played today.

Jimmy Morris, now remembered only as Jimmy Driftwood, would become an important folk and country songwriter. His music remained in demand for the remainder of his life. While he cranked out a number of country and pop hits, none could top "The Battle of New Orleans."

"The Battle of New Orleans" was not written for love or money, but rather to develop interest and knowledge. For more than twenty years, this song did just that: it helped students learn about their country's history. Today, the song's certified status as gold record has all but erased the real reason it was written, but every time it is played, "The Battle of New Orleans," in its own colorful way, still informs as it entertains.

11

COLUMBIA THE GEM
OF THE OCEAN

*I*n 1843, noted American vocalist David T. Shaw felt he needed a song that would bring the crowd to its feet at each of his concert appearances. Over the years he had tried numerous folk and classical pieces, and while they had been well received, none of them had set the house afire. A keen observer of people, Shaw knew that the one universal trait that seemed to resonate in the hearts of all Americans was national pride. The singer had also noted that songs like "The Star-Spangled Banner" and "Hail Columbia" were usually greeted with tremendous enthusiasm each time they were played or sung. Probably inspired by the message he found in "Hail Columbia," Shaw attempted to write his own American anthem. Yet months later, as the fall leaves began to litter New England streets, the singer had managed only to scribble down a few rather awkward lines.

One evening, as he prepared for his role in a musical production, Shaw took time to visit with another actor about his concept for an original patriotic song. Thomas Becket listened intently to the singer, then offered to take a look at what Shaw had already completed. Though Becket tried not to show it, the lines that he read amused him. He would later write, "He [Shaw] had produced some patriotic lines, but I found them ungrammatical, and so deficient in measure as to be totally unfit to be adapted to music."

Shaw could probably sense Becket's lack of enthusiasm for the project, but as the singer needed help, he begged the other actor to try to rework his ideas. Becket took the few lines that Shaw had written home with him that evening and tossed them promptly in the wastebasket. As he lay down for bed, a tune leaped into his mind, as did a few lines of lyrics.

The next day Becket easily jotted down the verses for "Columbia the Gem of the Ocean." With its rousing tune and unique words, the actor felt, the song had all the earmarks of a popular piece. Becket figured that all he needed to fully capitalize on his inspiration was the right exposure. Because Shaw was a major musical star of the period, the actor took "Columbia" back to the singer. The men agreed to share publishing rights to the new song.

Shaw premiered the anthem at the Chestnut Street Theater in Philadelphia. As Becket had figured, the crowds vigorously responded to his work. Each night the audience jumped to its feet when Shaw began to sing "Columbia the Gem of the Ocean." Soon many were even singing along with him. It must have been the majesty and upbeat music, mixed with the number's strong patriotic theme, that made the number a hit, because in truth, the words did not really make a great deal of sense.

During the era when this song was written, a gem in the ocean was an island. As the United States was hardly an island, the first

O, Columbia! the gem of the
  ocean,
The home of the brave and the free,
The shrine of each patriot's devotion,
A world offers homage to thee.
Thy mandates make heroes
  assemble
When Liberty's form stands in
  view;
Thy banners make tyranny tremble

When borne by the Red, White and
  Blue!
When borne by the Red, White and
  Blue!
When borne by the Red, White and
  Blue!
Thy banners make tyranny tremble
When borne by the Red, White and
  Blue!

The wine cup, the wine cup bring
  hither,
And fill you it true to the brim!
May the wreaths they have won
  never wither,
Nor the star of their glory grow
  dim!
May the service united ne'er sever,
But they to their colors prove true!

The Army and Navy forever,
Three cheers for the red, white and
  blue,
Three cheers for the red, white and
  blue,
Three cheers for the red, white and
  blue,
The Army and Navy forever,
Three cheers for the red, white and
  blue.

line of Becket's work stood out as a glaring misstatement of fact. The description simply did not work. Yet no one seemed to let this little bit of misinformation stand in the way of the song's sweeping across America like a strong north wind. By December, stores were selling sheet music to "Columbia the Gem of the Ocean" as far away as New Orleans. That just happened to be where Thomas Becket was performing in the days just before and after Christmas 1843. This was to be a holiday season that the writer would never forget. Long before the character was created, Becket met the Grinch.

Picking up the newly printed sheet music, Becket noticed that Shaw had taken sole credit for writing the new American favorite. Needless to say, the actor was enraged. With each sale of the sheet music, he was being cheated out of money. Returning to Philadelphia, Becket served Shaw and the publisher with a notice, and soon "Columbia" had all the makings of a gem of a lawsuit. Eventually, in a settlement reached out of court, Becket did receive writing credit.

Four years later, a Philadelphian who had heard Shaw sing "Columbia the Gem of the Ocean" was traveling in London and noted the familiar strains of Becket's song coming from a theater. There, on the English stage, E. L. Davenport was singing the tune, but this version was called "Britannia the Gem of the Ocean." When confronted with the fact that his song was being used in England, but with different words, the English-born Becket acknowledged that he might have heard the melody as a child. But he then claimed that Davenport must have rewritten the words for British audiences.

In truth, "Britannia" was probably being sung long before Shaw debuted "Columbia." After all, the British Isles really were the "gems of the ocean" at that time, so Becket must have lifted the words and music from the original English anthem. This would explain how he had composed the number so quickly and why he had called America a "gem." Yet even though the actor's inspiration for the song now seemed tainted, the number still remained popular in the United States.

The popularity of "Columbia the Gem of the Ocean" reached its zenith during the Civil War. In the 1860s, any song that spoke of patriotism and love of country was embraced with a fervor rarely seen today. And "Columbia," with its easy-to-remember words and tune, was probably the most performed anthem of the period. Up until the time, almost two decades later, when John Philip Sousa took over the Marine Band, this song was even the famed military orchestra's most requested number.

Soon after it was first published, Shaw lost all rights to "Columbia." He died almost forgotten. During one of his extended stays in England, Becket's rights were sold out from under him to a Baltimore publishing firm. Perhaps realizing that his claim to the song was shaky at best, when he returned to his adopted country the actor did not file a suit to regain his royalties.

Even though it is not performed as frequently as it was even two generations ago, "Columbia the Gem of the Ocean," thanks in part to the fact that it was always played during Popeye's fights with Bluto, remains one of the nation's most recognized anthems. Almost everyone can either hum the tune or recall a few lines from the old standard. And maybe today, when the United States reigns as the world's only remaining superpower, the line "Thy banners make tyranny tremble" is truer than ever before.

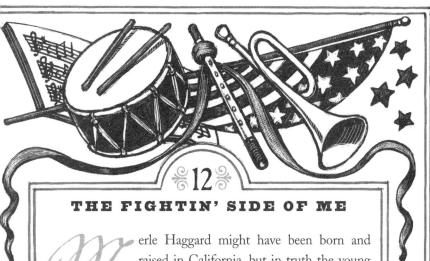

12

THE FIGHTIN' SIDE OF ME

*M*erle Haggard might have been born and raised in California, but in truth the young man was really an Oklahoman. Though he spent very little time in the red dirt of the old Indian Territory, he still carried both the insecurities and the values of a farm boy. Having migrated from Oklahoma in an attempt to survive the depression, the Haggard family, who lived in an old boxcar when Merle was born in 1937, could well have been the stars of Steinbeck's great novel *The Grapes of Wrath.* Merle's father died when the boy was in grade school, and Haggard grew up dirt poor, enduring the scorn of those who viewed any migrant laborer, brown, black, or white, as little more than dirt. With so little promise for the future and almost no hope in the present, it is not surprising that the young man dropped out of high school and ran away from home. After bumming up and down the West Coast, Haggard finally obtained a permanent address when he ended up in San Quentin Prison for burglary. At the age of twenty, Haggard was anything but the American hero.

Music became Haggard's salvation. Behind bars he wrote songs about his experiences, his emotions, and his hard luck. His first receptive audience was his fellow convicts. In 1960, when he was released after almost three years in prison, Haggard went back to his hometown of Bakersfield, California, to try to reclaim his life and his pride. While the city might not have been kind to the singer's family during the depression, it would now open the door of opportunity to the ex-con.

Thanks to Buck Owens, Bakersfield had become a mecca for country music—some even called the city "Nashville West." It was in this California town that Capitol Records first heard Merle Haggard. In 1965, just five years after he was released from jail, the label signed the young man to a recording contract. Unlike many who spent years trying to land a hit, the talented Haggard quickly found his place in Music City. His autobiographical third single, "I'm a Lonesome Fugitive," hit the top of the charts. Nine of his next dozen singles would also land at number 1. By the age of thirty, Merle Haggard was one of the most awarded and successful stars in the entertainment industry.

Haggard had a unique feel for the heart of the workingman and -woman. His music spoke directly to them. He seemed to be able to lyrically paint the common American's emotions, dreams, hopes, and fears in words as easily as Norman Rockwell had with a brush and canvas. Because Haggard's success came during one of the most volatile times in American history, the singer needed this kind of empathetic ability to relate to his often stressed-out fans. And he really knew how they felt too.

As he toured the nation, Haggard saw firsthand the divisions that frightened millions. As a man who had once rebelled against poverty and prejudice, the singer could strongly identify with the so-called antiestablishment. Like them he treasured freedom and wanted the American Dream for all Americans. Yet as a person who had been given a second chance by the system, he also felt a strong sense of loyalty to the country, its history, and its traditions. So, just like the nation, Haggard himself had reasons to be divided. Simply put, the musician was one of the few who saw both sides of the era's explosive political issues.

As Haggard was riding the nation's playlists and singing before larger and larger crowds, Lyndon Johnson gave way to Richard Nixon, and with the change in power, Americans seemed to grow even more cynical. The civil rights movement and the Vietnam War had drawn broad lines between races and ages, and millions from a confused generation of baby boomers rebelled against society and their parents by getting involved in drugs, sex, and alternate lifestyles. The once unthinkable was now everyday life as whole sections of cities were set on fire, students were shot by National Guardsmen, draft cards were burned in front of courthouses, and mass murderers killed people just for thrills. No one could make sense out of this cultural revolution. As he toured the nation on his bus, Merle and his band got to see all this confusion and pain up close.

When passing long hours on the road, Haggard and his band often had heated political discussions. They might have played the same music, but they were not all on the same side of the political fence. One day, just outside of Muskogee, Oklahoma, someone offered the opinion "I bet that they don't smoke marijuana here in Muskogee." Haggard laughed and immediately listed some other things that they probably didn't do in central Oklahoma. Out of that simple discussion grew one of the biggest hits in the history of country music, "Okie from Muskogee."

In this song, Haggard basically stated, "Yes, I am proud to be an Okie. And even if America has done me wrong and kicked me around a bit, I am proud to be an American too." The record would become the Country Music Association's Single of the Year in 1969.

If anything, "Okie from Muskogee" was a novelty song. Haggard had written it to be humorous. While it did uncover and reveal the emotions of millions who were tired of the cultural revolution that had so divided Americans, it was more a snapshot of the way things used to be than how they should be. So rather than "Okie," it would be the next song Haggard released that would become one of the most-played flag-waving numbers of that or any other era.

As Haggard watched the nightly news, he saw a number of things that deeply disturbed him. Though he believed that every American had the right to protest and freely voice opinions in opposition to the government, Haggard had great reservations about those who burned flags or spoke ill of the men who had accepted the call and were fighting for the United States in Vietnam. He believed that just because the war was unpopular didn't mean that the men who had been sent to fight battles should be ridiculed and called murderers.

As the divisions created by Vietnam grew deeper, Haggard watched the generations often come to blows in front of courthouses, schools, and draft boards, and even at his concerts. It was unsettling to say the least. As he had with almost every facet of his own life, the singer-songwriter began to look for a way to voice his concerns in music. What would come out of Haggard's creative mind would be more than a hit song; the lyrics would spawn millions of bumper stickers and would fuel scores of congressional campaigns.

While "Okie from Muskogee" might have been just another country song, "The Fightin' Side of Me" was an anthem. It was immediately embraced not only by those who were a part of the country music market, but by conservative city folks who had been searching for a modern song that voiced their anger at the way the rebellious youth were behaving. For those who had survived the depression, who had fought on the war fronts or supported the U.S. effort at home during World War II, and for those who had earned a piece of the American Dream during the 1950s, "The Fightin' Side of Me" carried a message that fully voiced their anger. While those who embraced "Fightin'" did not march in the streets, they still wanted to be heard. In a very real sense, they felt that their opinions were being trumpeted every time Haggard sang his song.

President Nixon, who seemed like anything but a country music fan, latched onto "The Fightin' Side of Me." He even invited Haggard and his band to come to the White House and sing it. For many in Congress, it became a campaign ballad. Across the United States hundreds of thousands transformed one line of the song into a bumper sticker: "America—Love It or Leave It." Haggard's version of red, white, and blue had created more than a craze; it had started a movement that some called "angry" patriotism.

With "Okie" and "The Fightin' Side of Me," Merle Haggard joined Bob Hope as America's highest-profile patriot. Though he had probably never intended for it to happen, the ex-con was now being draped in the flag. When he ended his shows with those two flag-waving hits, crowds went into a frenzy. Flags appeared out of nowhere, people rose to their feet en masse, many saluted, some cried, and almost everyone sang along with the star.

As he moved through 1970, Haggard began to become uncomfortable with his new image as the spokesperson for conservative America. At many of his concerts, picketers now showed up. They accused him of being a puppet for President Nixon, J. Edgar Hoover, and a host of other established leaders. Haggard easily spoke of the breaks that he had been given by the nation, but even he did not believe the government had a free pass to do whatever it wanted. While he despised seeing an American flag being burned, he also thought that those who disagreed with what was going on in the United States had a right to be heard as well.

"A lot of people might have misinterpreted those songs," Haggard observed. "I'm not saying you can't stand up and say what you believe in. That's one of the most important rights we have, and that is what I'm doing. But I am saying—and I am attacking—anything that might destroy democracy."

Haggard would also note that he lost many college-age fans when the song came out. That was something he hated. Coming from a rebellious background, he related very well to the problems and challenges that faced many of the nation's youth. Yet having seen firsthand what happened when one broke the law, he did not want anyone else to have to spend time paying for mistakes in judgment in a jail cell.

In a move that showed his convictions and his courage, even with "The Fightin' Side of Me" still in rotation on radio playlists, Haggard began to back away from its message. Merle also separated himself from a wide number of groups, including presidential candidate George Wallace, who wanted to use him and his music for their own brand of Americanism. At concerts and in press conferences, the singer voiced his own concerns about racial problems and social programs. While he praised the men who fought in Vietnam, he admitted that he did not understand why American troops were being asked to give their lives for this cause. His fans soon discovered that many of Haggard's thoughts were far more liberal and tolerant than theirs. Yet like his music, his words made people think and examine their own views and opinions.

Merle Haggard would go on to become one of the greatest entertainers in the history of music. A legend in his time, he proved that the American Dream could work for anyone. This ex-con, who in 1970 wrote the most popular anthem for the "silent majority," also penned some of the most sensitive and beautiful songs ever released in country music. "The Fightin' Side of Me" found a place in music and national history during some of the most turbulent times in the twentieth century, yet it might be even better suited for a day when this nation has become the symbol of democracy for the whole world. In the twenty-first century, the United States finds itself in a world where Haggard's song is less about protest and more about reality, and those who used to protest against Merle and his lyrics now sing "The Fightin' Side of Me" with him.

❧13❧

GOD BLESS AMERICA

*T*he legendary Irving Berlin has been hailed by music experts as the greatest songwriter in American history. If he were still alive, the highly competitive and self-assured tune master would probably agree with this assessment and point to his huge body of work as proof that he was head and shoulders above Gershwin, Cohan, and all the other giants of American composition. Berlin, who died in 1989 at 101, created a long list of classics that spanned almost the entire last century. From his first huge hit, "Alexander's Ragtime Band," to "White Christmas" to "There's No Business Like Show Business," his hundreds of tunes and scores of chart toppers made Berlin a household name for more than seventy years. While his career would have been no less remarkable without "God Bless America," it was this song, one that the composer himself had once dismissed, that would become the small Russian immigrant's greatest gift to his adopted country.

In 1918, Berlin, the son of a Jewish cantor, found himself

in the United States Army. Though he had been the toast of Broadway for several years, he had only become a citizen a few weeks before he was drafted. He spent his first few months in the service stationed at Long Island's Camp Upton. Though the war was winding down and there was little chance the Allies would need the almost thirty-year-old man for action at the front, the songwriter nevertheless hated the demands and routine of army life. He longed to be back on Broadway, creating songs that an entire nation would sing. When the army private heard George M. Cohan's "Over There," Berlin came up with an idea that would put him in charge of his own fate and take him back to the Great White Way.

Just before Berlin was scheduled to be shipped out to France to help American forces put the final nail in imperial Germany's coffin, he convinced the army brass to allow him to write and produce a Broadway show using a cast composed entirely of "real" soldiers. The production, which described a comedic side of military life from an enlisted man's point of view, was called *Yip! Yip! Yaphank!* It would become a hit at New York's Century Theater and be used as a fundraiser for the war effort, and it would quickly elevate Berlin to the rank of sergeant.

Berlin, whose unbridled love of America might have been tied to his own incredible success, had originally written a very uplifting patriotic number for the show. The melody finished, the words in an almost final stage, the song was meant to be the big closer. Yet the more the master tunesmith studied the still-unnamed ballad, the more he became convinced it didn't work. The doughboys, as World War I soldiers were called, had a reputation for being fun-loving, irreverent clowns. Many of them were poor rural kids who took every opportunity that came their way to party. With this in mind,

Berlin couldn't see how these men could connect to the syrupy flag-waving standard he had just completed. Besides, he told his secretary, there had already been too many patriotic songs unleashed on the public during the war years. America didn't need another one. Deeming his creation forgettable, the writer pulled the song, placed it in a file, and forgot about it altogether.

At about the same time *Yip! Yip! Yaphank!* was making its stage debut, a nine-year-old girl from the Blue Ridge Mountains was singing at a bond rally in her current hometown, Washington, D.C. On this night in 1916 little Kate Smith was stealing the show. When she pounded out a stirring rendition of "Over There," she touched even General John J. "Blackjack" Pershing. The officer was so moved that he wangled the child a visit to the White House. Within a week, the president had dined with the youngster, given her a medal as a way of thanking her for her bond-raising efforts, and encouraged her to continue to use her vocal talents. Smith took those words to heart.

Kate kept a busy performance schedule at a local theater through high school, but when she graduated she gave up singing and entered Georgetown University to study nursing. Still, the no longer little Smith yearned for the stage. In 1926, at the age of nineteen, she quit school and landed a singing gig at the Earle Theater. Her rotund size made her the butt of cruel jokes by comics and the audience. There were many nights she left the stage humiliated and in tears. Though heartbroken by the pointed jabs and catcalls, she wouldn't give up. By 1929, Kate Smith's voice and smile had made her a Broadway star and landed her a recording contract with Columbia Records. Though still the victim of many jokes, at 260 pounds, the young woman with the big voice was an established New York stage act.

As a child Smith had written a poem about a moon coming over a mountain. Her manager and Columbia record executive Ted Collins gave Smith's composition to two established songwriters, Harry Woods and Howard Johnson. "When the Moon Comes Over the Mountain" would become one of the biggest hit songs of 1931. At the same time that her record was climbing the charts, Smith was offered her own radio program on CBS. Her sweet, sincere personality, coupled with her lusty, robust voice, quickly made the songstress one of radio's most popular stars. Hollywood even called, putting the radio and recording star into a series of musical shorts.

The marriage between Kate Smith and radio was still going strong in 1937, when she began searching for a special number to perform on her Armistice Day broadcast. She wanted something new and patriotic to sing as a gift to the families of those who had lost loved ones in World War I, as well as to the troops who had come back home after serving in that conflict. As Smith had a very loyal following among veterans who remembered her performances for the doughboys during the war, finding just the right number was of paramount importance to her. Even though the search began months ahead of the scheduled program date, two weeks before the air date, nothing she found had grabbed her interest. Ironically, the man who had a song that could fit her need was half a world away.

Irving Berlin visited London in the late summer and early fall of 1938. The talk of war was epidemic in England, and the songwriter couldn't escape the constant news of what many felt was an inevitable conflict. When he returned home to New York in Octo-

ber, Berlin escaped the atmosphere of distress and worry he had discovered in Europe, but he could not leave behind his own fears about
another pending global war.

Berlin felt the answer to his angst was to pen a new song that
embraced a theme of peace. He somehow believed that if he could
write a hit on this theme, he might be able to help his country stay
out of the next world war. Initially he went to work on a number
called "Thanks, America." When he failed to complete that song, he
tried his hand at "Let's Talk About Liberty." Neither attempt produced results that Berlin felt would be commercial. Yet he would not
give up. He continued to burn the midnight oil, pound away at his
piano, and put pen to paper in an effort to answer what he felt was
almost a divine calling.

As a frustrated Berlin played with a variety of ideas, Ted Collins
stopped by the Berlin Music Company. Smith's manager wanted to
know if the famed composer had anything on file that Kate could
use for her Armistice Day salute. As the writer considered Smith's
largely rural fan base and her long list of sentimental hits, he thought
back to the untitled number he had cut out of *Yip! Yip! Yaphank!* It
might have taken the songwriter's secretary several hours to find the
original lyrics in a long-forgotten file locked in an old trunk, but it
took Berlin only a few minutes to rewrite, update, and title "God
Bless America."

As soon as she heard it, Kate Smith immediately loved the gushy
ballad. As a woman of faith, she grabbed onto the song's introduction
as if it were a prayer. Yes, she must have thought when she first sang
the words, storm clouds are gathering across the sea, but with God's
help, we can either avoid this conflict or find a way to survive it.

As the days ticked down to the song's radio debut, a couple of lyrical changes were made. Berlin had originally written one of the song's key lines as "Through the right, with the light from above." As all things "right" were now considered socialist or communist in nature, "right" was change to "night." Another rewrite was necessary to remove a reference to Americans fighting in a war. "Make her victorious on land and foam" became "from the green fields of Virginia to the gold fields of Nome."

Smith, who took every opportunity to tug at the heart strings, didn't perform the song but still found a way to initially spotlight "God Bless America" on her afternoon program *Kate Smith Speaks*. On the CBS broadcast she informed her audience that that night's *Kate Smith Hour* was going to include something very special.

"When I first tried [to sing] it ['God Bless America'] over," Smith explained, "I felt, here is a song that will be timeless—it will never die—others will thrill to its beauty long after we are gone. In my humble estimation, this is the greatest song Irving Berlin has ever composed. It shall be my happy privilege to introduce that song on my program this evening, dedicating it to our American heroes of the world war. As I stand before the microphone and sing it with all my heart, I'll be thinking of our veterans and I'll be praying with every breath I draw that we shall never have another war."

At 12:13 A.M. eastern time, the Songbird of the South strolled to her CBS microphone, took a deep breath, and said, "And now it is my very great privilege to sing you a song that's never been sung before by anybody, and that was written especially for me by one of the greatest composers in the music field today. It's something more than a song—I feel it's one of the most beautiful compositions ever written, a song that will never die. The author: Mr. Irving Berlin. The title: 'God Bless America.'"

Smith might have intentionally stretched the truth when she stated that "God Bless America" had been written especially for her, or Collins and Berlin might have led her to believe that it had been composed with her mind, but either way, the song that had once been considered too schmaltzy for release was an immediate hit. Nick Kenny would write in the *New York Sunday Mirror*, "I wonder if I ever received as big a thrill as I did last Thursday listening to Kate Smith's inspiring singing of Irving Berlin's new patriotic hymn." Millions must have felt the same way. Within minutes of Smith's sincere and moving performance, CBS's switchboard was flooded. Within twenty-four hours, hundreds of thousands of requests for records and sheet music were received by Columbia and Berlin Music. President Franklin Roosevelt commented on it; it was the talk on street corners, in barbershops, schools, churches, and city halls in every part of the United States.

Before the music presses began to print copies of "God Bless America," Berlin went back to work fine-tuning it. The songwriter rewrote "From the green fields of Virginia to the gold fields of Nome" to "From the mountains, to the valleys, to the oceans white with foam." Meanwhile, Smith reworked her arrangement to change its military-march-style cadence to a pure ballad. This new and now familiar version of the song was first heard on Kate's program on November 24, 1938.

"God Bless America" touched so many that within months millions demanded that the government toss out "The Star-Spangled Banner" and use Berlin's song as the new national anthem. Congress discussed it, and the president was even asked to comment on it. This action was so seriously considered that the song's lyrics were placed in the national record. Smith, though flattered, came out against this movement. Two years later she even recorded "The Star-Spangled Banner" on the flip side of "God Bless America" to help defuse the debate. Berlin also voiced support for Francis Scott Key's ode to the American flag.

Though it did not replace "The Star-Spangled Banner," "God Bless America" quickly became the nation's most popular patriotic song. And while scores of artists, including Bing Crosby and Gene Autry, recorded it, the song would become the signature number of the large woman with the even larger radio following. Smith would sing it at countless bond rallies during World War II, and at thousands of concerts, and would reprise her introduction of "God Bless America" in the 1943 movie *This Is the Army*.

At the end of the war in 1945, most of the patriotic standards of the era disappeared, yet Smith's "God Bless America" did not. It became a staple at sporting events, political conventions, and holiday festivals. Long after her radio days ended, the song kept Kate Smith in the public eye.

During the sixties, old-fashioned patriotic fervor gave way to Vietnam War protest. Not surprisingly, "God Bless America" was not heard as often. In the early 1970s, the National Hockey League's Philadelphia Flyers changed all that. As a way of trying to keep their fans interested, the team's management began to alternate Smith's "God Bless America" with "The Star-Spangled Banner." Not only did the Flyer fans like "God Bless America" better, but it seemed to inspire the team as well. They rarely lost when Smith's recording was played. On October 11, 1973, Smith sang the song in person in front of 17,007 fans. The standing ovation she received as she appeared on the ice lasted more than five minutes and delayed the start of the game. Kate repeated the performance before the May 12, 1974,

Stanley Cup playoff game against the Boston Bruins. The Flyers easily locked up the championship that night and called the singer the series MVP. With the game covered by the national media, Smith's star again rose, and her recordings resurfaced on radio stations and at record outlets. Two years later, during the Bicentennial celebrations, "God Bless America" was the song of choice at almost every major event.

It would be a Canadian, Celine Dion, who would usher "God Bless America" into the twenty-first century. Dion performed the song at a benefit for victims in the days after the tragic events of September 11, 2001. At a time of great national anguish, fear, and trial, Irving Berlin's composition would again inspire a nation.

Two years after its initial release, the *New York Times* asked Berlin why "God Bless America" had become such a national favorite. He told the paper, "The reason 'God Bless America' caught on is that it happens to have a universal appeal."

"God Bless America" is often called the unofficial national anthem of the United States. It seems that as long as there is a USA, the song will be cherished. When the song was first sung to a national audience in 1938 it created chills as it inspired a depression-weary nation. Now, seven decades later, there can be little doubt that, as Kate Smith said before its debut, it is a song that will never die. Still, it is ironic that a song once deemed not good enough for a Broadway show, a number that was lost for two decades in a file and then recorded by a woman who was often the butt of jokes, has evolved into the nation's most beloved patriotic anthem. As Berlin once told a reporter, "Songs make history and sometimes history makes songs." It the case of "God Bless America," it might work both ways.

14

GOD BLESS THE U.S.A.

*L*ee Greenwood is an American institution. He has entertained presidents, kings, queens, millions of country music fans, and hundreds of thousands of American servicemen and -women. His hit songs include such country music classics as "I.O.U.," "Dixie Road," "Mornin' Ride," and "To Me." Greenwood has twice been named the Country Music Association's Male Vocalist of the Year and is one of the most versatile stage performers in the entertainment industry. Yet it was one song released in 1984 that didn't top the charts that put the singer-songwriter on the American music map forever. It moved him from being a country music heartthrob to being one of this nation's most loved patriotic icons. This anthem, inspired by an international tragedy, was almost dismissed before it was recorded and probably would never have been released to the American public if Greenwood hadn't hand delivered it to the head of his record label. The fact that it now seems that everyone knows the words to "God Bless the U.S.A." is a tribute as much to the American tradition of going against established thinking as it is to the message of the song itself.

Success did not come easily for Lee Greenwood. He was born on a farm just outside of Sacramento, California, in 1942. His father was a musician in the United States Navy. His mother played instruments as well. So it was natural that Lee would inherit some of his parents' talent and pick up a love for music. He formed his first band, the Moonbeams, during his high school days in Sacramento. By the time he finished his senior year, his musical talents were well recognized up and down the West Coast. Hungry for a life in the spotlight, Greenwood turned down a musical scholarship at the College of the Pacific. Rather than getting a degree, he opted to gamble his future by performing in Reno, Nevada. Dreaming of overnight success in rock and roll, the young man would spend almost two decades as a lounge act, talented enough to open for some of the biggest stars in the world, but never given the break he needed to establish himself as a real player in the world of show business.

By the late sixties, Greenwood's confidence in America had been sharply tested. The war in Vietnam; the assassinations of John Kennedy, Martin Luther King Jr., and Bobby Kennedy; race riots; and his own career setbacks had left him shaken. He naturally put his emotions into a song. This song seemed to echo many of the thoughts Woody Guthrie had once written into the original antigovernment protest version of "This Land Is Your Land." Greenwood would perform his "America" during his concert sets. Yet though it questioned some of the established thinking of the time, unlike many of the protest songs of that era, this new look at the national scene didn't completely give up on the American Dream. In "America," Lee forecast a nation that would come to terms with its problems and would successfully deal with the issues that confronted it. "America," with its honest views and optimistic ending, might well have been an important ballad for that era, if only Greenwood had been able to secure a national recording gig. As it was, this song, like most of the others the singer sang in Vegas and Reno, was enjoyed, then forgotten by those who caught his act.

By 1978, after almost eighteen years of false starts, Greenwood gave up on his dreams of rock fame and took his smoky voice to Nashville to try his luck with country. Jerry Crutchfield, then head of MCA Publishing, liked what he heard during an audition and signed Greenwood. Three years later, just short of his fortieth birthday, Lee was an "overnight" success. He was voted the Country Music Association's Male Vocalist of the Year, won a Grammy for Best Country Vocal Performance, and locked up a gold album. But while this assured his status as a country music entertainer and justified his more than two decades of hard work playing in clubs, it would be a tragic international incident that would inspire him to compose a timeless song that would speak to and for tens of millions of Americans.

On September 1, 1983, a Korean Air Lines flight with the ironic designation 007 was shot down off the Russian coast by a USSR jet fighter. All 269 people, including 63 Americans, would die in the attack. A United States spy plane had been flying in the same area as the Korean Air Lines flight that evening, and the Soviet fighter had somehow mistaken the commercial jet, which had accidentally veered into Russian airspace, for the military plane. It took only one missile to bring the airliner down.

As the media reported the incident, shock echoed up and down streets on both sides of the Pacific. In government chambers and in the homes of those who had seen loved ones die for no reason, people asked why. In Japan the tragedy had an individual face, as millions mourned the loss of a recording star. Kyu Sakamoto had become the first Japanese singer to top the American pop charts when, in 1963, he scored a number 1 record with "Sukiyaki." The performer was one of those who had been killed. In the United States, where the victims were not as well known, the brutality of the act would keep the story on front pages for weeks and toss the government back into a cold war mentality.

Lee Greenwood would later say that initially the events confused him. He simply could not believe an accident like this could happen in a modern world. A few days after the attack, the songwriter put pen to paper and tried to record his thoughts. It would be one of the easiest pieces he would ever write. He did not tell the story of the crash; rather, he wrote about his own love of his native land and why he felt blessed to be an American.

Greenwood's unswerving loyalty and sentimentality would have seemed out of place a few years before. Yet the attack on flight 007 had united a nation, and the timing of his simple message was perfect for an era when Ronald Reagan was in the White House and American flags were again being flown with great pride on the country's streets. Now, with patriotic fever running so high, all that was left for the singer to do was record "God Bless the U.S.A." and release it to the American public. This would seem to have been an easy assignment, but in fact it would take some time and arm-twisting.

Jerry Crutchfield liked the song the first time he heard it, but recommended that Greenwood rewrite the second verse to include references to specific American locations—much as had been done in "America the Beautiful." After he had rewritten and revised "God Bless the U.S.A.," Greenwood took the song to his label, MCA. Most of those in power in Music City felt that the song, which did not have a solid country feel, should not be recorded by the song's writer. They advised Greenwood that he needed to stick to the formula that had made him a star. His career was too new to take chances. It was suggested that he even give the composition to someone else to record, an artist who was established and could take a chance on a different kind of song.

In spite of what he was told, Greenwood would not give up on "God Bless the U.S.A." He had performed it on several occasions and the response he had received from his country music audiences had been incredible. He simply knew that given an opportunity, it would work commercially. While in Los Angeles on business in the fall of the year, Greenwood took the song directly to MCA Records president Irving Azoff. Azoff liked it but didn't want to immediately cut or release it. He did promise Greenwood that the singer could record it when the label put together material for his next album. In other words, "God Bless the U.S.A" would be an album cut, but not a single.

In early 1984, Greenwood put the finishing touches on *You've Got a Good Love Comin'*. As promised, one of the songs he recorded for that album was "God Bless the U.S.A." When Irving Azoff heard the ten songs on the new disk, he reversed his original thinking and ordered the label to give the patriotic tune a try as a single. It seemed that Azoff had a hunch.

Though it might seem hard to believe now, "God Bless the U.S.A." was not a smash hit; it did not make an impact on the pop or rock charts and only hit number 7 on the country playlists. In a sense, the experts in Nashville had been proven right too. After this release Greenwood's country record sales were put into a bit of spin. It would take four releases and more than a year before he would hit number 1 again. Yet even though "God Bless the U.S.A." did not race up the *Billboard* charts, it did strike a chord with millions of Americans. They might not have rushed out to the stores to buy the single or album, but they wanted to hear the song so badly that it quickly became a staple at local ball games, amateur shows, and school presentations. And long after "God Bless the U.S.A." had left the charts, it was still being used at political rallies, veterans salutes, and even grocery store openings. Thanks to this groundswell, a host of other recording artists picked up the song, recorded it, and sang in their shows. As it turned out, that was just the beginning.

Ronald Reagan latched onto the song as a part of his reelection campaign in 1984. George Bush Sr. rode "God Bless the U.S.A." to the presidency in 1988. Because of these two campaigns, "God Bless the U.S.A." was so closely identified with the Republican Party that it might have become more political than patriotic if it had not been for a dictator in Iraq. When America responded to Iraq's invasion of Kuwait, General Norman Schwarzkopf announced that Greenwood's anthem would be the theme song for the Persian Gulf War. Within four years of its release, thanks in large part to Schwarzkopf, "God Bless the U.S.A." had become a new generation's "God Bless America."

In the aftermath of the events of September 11, 2001, "God Bless the U.S.A." moved beyond music. The number's title was used on bumper stickers, buttons, T-shirts, and billboards. It and "God Bless America" became the anthems that helped present a united front and the strength of American determination to the whole world.

The songwriter had bucked the advice of the experts and taken a career risk in releasing "God Bless the U.S.A.," and the results reflected as much about what was still right about the country as did the words. Lee Greenwood lived the American Dream and then gave his thanks in a song that will be sung and remembered long after the singer and the events that inspired "God Bless the U.S.A." are but a distant memory.

❦15❧

HAIL COLUMBIA

*I*n 1794, America was falling apart at the seams. A war between France and Britain had created a chasm that many felt was going to bring the fledgling nation to its knees. Congress was deeply divided as to which of the warring countries would gain U.S. support. The Republicans were opposed to the Jay Treaty, which favored England. Yet the anti-French group, made up mainly of Federalists, pushed the treaty through and made it the law of the land. As soon as the president signed that treaty, a new round of debates was initiated to overturn the legislation. With furious denunciations, name-calling, and dirty political plays, the two parties would battle over this dilemma for the next four years. Then, in 1798, rather than burying the hachet and getting on with American business, another bill was passed that even more inflamed almost half the nation's population.

The Federal Party controlled Congress, and in a move that many viewed as being anti-American, the Federalists passed the Alien and Sedition Acts. These new laws allowed the president to banish anyone he personally felt did not meet the requirements for being a loyal American. For many, these laws had the potential to make the nation a monarchy or dictatorship. They certainly paved a route for a president using law to rid himself of anyone he viewed as a political enemy. In many ways the Alien and Sedition Acts made the nation's chief executive judge, jury, and executioner. Because of these laws and what they stood for, resentfulness and hatred were at an all time high in the capital. Each day the breach between Federalists and Republicans grew wider. Some even feared a civil war.

In modern American politics, those from opposing parties who battle it out on the floors of the House and Senate often dine or play golf together as friends later in the day. In the late 1700s, political enemies not only didn't take supper with members of the other party, they would occasionally challenge each other to duels. It would not have been surprising to see Federalist and Republican congressmen locked in a wrestling match just outside the legislative chambers. So as the war between England and France continued, the warring between parties in Philadelphia, America's capital city at that time, grew worse.

As the division in America ripped the City of Brotherly Love down party lines, Gilbert Fox prepared for an engagement at one of the Philadephia's best theaters. Fox knew that the climate for his debut was hardly ideal. Conditions were so volatile that Fox had been warned that any song he sang could very well inflame those who came to see him perform. It was prudently suggested that he removed all English and French tunes from his program. But because America was still a very young country and so had not yet inspired much original music, Fox realized that if he removed all

Hail! Columbia, happy land!
Hail! ye heroes, heaven-born band,
Who fought and bled in freedom's
	cause,
And when the storm of war was gone,
Enjoyed the peace your valor won;

Let independence be your boast,
Ever mindful what it cost,
Ever grateful for the prize,
Let its altar reach the skies.

Firm, united let us be,
Rallying round our liberty,
As a band of brothers joined,
Peace and safety we shall find.

Immortal patriots, rise once more!
Defend your rights, defend your
	shore;
Let no rude foe with impious hand,
Invade the shrine where sacred lies
Of toil and blood the well-earned
	prize;

While offering peace, sincere and
	just,
In heaven we place a manly trust,
That truth and justice will prevail,
And every scheme of bondage fail.

Sound, sound the trump of fame!
Let Washington's great name
Ring through the world with loud
	applause!
Let every clime to freedom dear
Listen with a joyful ear;

With equal skill, with steady
	power,
He governs in the fearful hour
Of horrid war, or guides with ease
The happier time of honest
	peace.

Behold the chief, who now com-
	mands,
Once more to serve his country
	stands,
The rock on which the storm will
	beat!
But armed in virtue, firm and true,
His hopes are fixed on heaven and
	you.

When hope was sinking in dismay,
When gloom obscured Columbia's
	day,
His steady mind, from changes
	free,
Resolved on death or liberty.

songs that had been written by composers from the two warring nations, then there were very few songs left for him to sing. At a loss as to how to proceed, the young man turned to a trusted friend, Joseph Hopkinson.

It was April 1798 when Fox knocked on Hopkinson's door. On that Saturday afternoon the two men began their visit by talking about politics and the dismal mood of most who lived in the city. The singer then asked Hopkinson, who was a lawyer, if he knew of any patriotic song that might appeal to both Federalists and Republicans. With the nation just over two decades old, the catalog for songs was rather limited, so the lawyer offered to try to compose something for the performance. Fox not only accepted the offer, but begged the lawyer to come up with a song that very night.

As he considered the job he had volunteered to attempt, Hopkinson began to review music to which he could set his lyrics. It was a common practice during this time for songwriters simply to borrow familiar tunes. Some songs had as many as three hundred different sets of lyrics that had been coupled to their melodies. So almost any tune that he knew was available to the lawyer for use. Hopkinson probably considered hymns, classical odes, and folk songs before settling on a tune that had been written in 1789 by a German American named Phylo. It had first been played at George Washington's inauguration and had thus earned the name "President's March." As most in the nation still had warm feelings for the first president, Hopkinson decided to use the song most identified with Washington as the base on which to mount his new lyrics. With this music as a framework, the lawyer then carefully considered what his words should say.

Hopkinson worked with the text of his new song's verses as carefully as he would have any of the summations for his trials. In this case he knew that the rather large and boisterous jury that would hear his friend sing would be much more forceful and less forgiving than any judge or jury of the day. He also figured that the only way he might be able to please both sides was by appealing not to their political instincts, but to their sense of national pride. Thus, Hopkinson searched for phrases that would unite, while excluding anything that might be divisive. He carefully studied each word and line, trying to uncover and eliminate hidden meanings or agendas that politicians could use to foster ill feelings. When he was satisfied that his new work was completely politically neutral, he again met with Fox. Fox loved the new song, but he wondered if those who paid to hear him sing would simply view "Hail Columbia" as another facet of this extended and mean-spirited national debate. It was said that the singer spent more time in prayer than he did actually learning the words and melody to his friend's song.

A nervous Fox took the stage on his first evening and looked out at a packed house. He was astute enough to note that the Republicans were largely sitting on one side of the theater and those loyal to the Federalists were on the other. Sweat poured from his brow as Fox valiantly made it from one song to the next, carefully watching to see if his choices had set off the first shot in another political war. Finally, about halfway through the performance, he decided to sing the new number that had been penned for the occasion by Hopkinson.

Fox began quietly, but his voice grew stronger with each note and word. As he majestically worked his way through the initial stanza and began the final lines of the initial stanza, he felt a change in the overall attitude of the audience. For the first time this evening, they were not as much judging as they were listening. They were also hanging on each note and word. By the time he concluded the final verse, the frowns that had seemed permanently etched on the crowd's faces a few minutes before had turned to smiles. Some of the men were crying. As one, without regard to party, they rose, cheering and demanding an encore. Fox obliged, and the response was the same. For the next half hour the only song that the theater patrons would accept was "Hail Columbia." By night's end, the throng was joining the singer in a lusty rendition that could be heard blocks away.

The new song seemed to have an immediate healing effect on Congress. The party politics were still evident, but the next day both sides talked more about how to fix the nation's problems than attempt to divide each issue along party lines. "Hail Columbia" was indeed a tonic the country needed.

Two days after Fox first performed Hopkinson's "Hail Columbia," President John Adams and every head of the various departments of the United States government showed up at the theater to hear this new song for themselves. After listening to it, Adams called for Fox to sing that song several more times. As the nation's leader got up to go home, the singer was saluted by Adams. It was gesture that shocked many of the theater's patrons. Yet no one could have predicted the shocking development that would happen just a few minutes later.

As President Adams and his delegation departed the theater, thousands of Americans lined the streets. In one voice this mass of humanity began to sing "Hail Columbia." Even Adams and members of Congress joined in. Perhaps there has never been such a spontaneous musical moment in American political history. As Hopkinson looked on, as he heard his words sung by thousands of different voices, he realized that his goal had been accomplished: he had written a song that united all of his countrymen. Perhaps inspired by this incident, the lawyer would spend the remainder of his life trying to maintain the ideal objectives he had set forth in his song.

For many years "Hail Columbia" was played when a president attended a formal dinner. It eventually lost its place as a presidential song to "Hail to the Chief." Yet the song, using one of the earliest nicknames for America, was not forgotten and is still used on a regular basis. Though first given an official nod by the nation's second president, "Hail Columbia" is now the anthem most often played to honor the vice president of the United States.

At a critical moment when it appeared that government "by the people and for the people" might not survive to see the 1800s, a Philadelphia singer and a young lawyer gave the country a musical peace offering. "Hail Columbia" united a divided nation and got two sides to talking about things that brought them together instead of tearing them apart. In the midst of a heated political war, Americans rediscovered a bit of this song's peace and unity. When they did, they forged ahead with a new vision of what America should and must be. Appropriately, one of the leaders of that movement would be Joseph Hopkinson, who would serve his country as both a federal judge and a member of Congress.

16

HAIL TO THE CHIEF

On July 4, 1828, the United States Marine Band greeted President John Quincy Adams with the tune "Hail to the Chief." Adams, who had departed from Washington to attend the official Independence Day groundbreaking for the C&O Canal, politely stood and listened to the familiar music, then, after the band had finished, went on with his official duties. Adams, as well as the thousands of others gathered that warm summer day, must have wondered why the marines had chosen that particular music. Though "Hail to the Chief" was a popular song during the period, it was not a song specifically associated with the office of president. In fact, during this period and for almost 150 years, there was not even a national anthem, much less a song solely designated for the country's chief executive. Hence, the playing of "Hail to the Chief" might never again have been associated with the office of president if local newspapers had not reported that the "airs from the Marine Band lightened the toil." Later, in some articles, buried beneath the names of local officials and reports of the day's weather, the song "Hail to the Chief" was mentioned and Adams was identified as the "Chief." Yet, as Adams might have known, the song that is now so closely identified with the president of the United States did not originate in America and was never intended to be used as a welcoming for a leader of any country. "Hail to the Chief" was actually inspired by the work of a knight of the British realm.

In the early 1800s, one of the most read and beloved English works of literature was written by Sir Walter Scott. His *The Lady of the Lake* was a best-selling poem in Great Britain. The ode was so popular that at least two different writers reworked it into a play. It is not known if Scott gave his permission for any of the live-performance versions of his epic, but he was aware of them. In 1810, he wrote a friend that "*The Lady of the Lake* is being made into a play by Martin and Reynolds in London and by a Mr. Siddons in Edinburgh."

Though there are no precise dates, "Hail to the Chief" must have been written in 1811. In one of the theatrical productions of *The Lady of the Lake,* James Sanderson pulled an idea for the song from a portion of canto 2. Later that year Scott received a letter from an army officer. That correspondence included the music to the "Boat Song" from the Sanderson play. This number was entitled "Hail to the Chief."

Since Americans were too busy building a nation to become immersed in developing a large theater movement, during the early nineteenth century hit plays in England quickly migrated across the Atlantic to New York. Anxious Americans could hardly wait to see the latest stage production from the old country. On May 8, 1812, only a year or so after it premiered in its land of origin, *The Lady of the Lake* made its American debut. Even though the United States

THE BEST-KNOWN AMERICAN LYRICS

Hail to the Chief we have chosen
for the nation,
Hail to the Chief! We salute him,
one and all.
Hail to the Chief, as we pledge
cooperation
In proud fulfillment of a great,
noble call.

Yours is the aim to make this grand
country grander,
This you will do, That's our strong,
firm belief.
Hail to the one we selected as com-
mander,
Hail to the President! Hail to the
Chief!

and Great Britain were beginning to fight the War of 1812, the play and the music taken from the production quickly became popular in New York, Boston, and up and down the Atlantic Coast. Taking advantage of the public's fascination with the musical, a host of publishers released a dozen different versions of "Hail to the Chief." It quickly became a best-seller.

As was common during this period, a number of different American lyrics were combined with the original English music. Some were serious, others parodies, and a few even attempted to tell the story of the American effort in the new war. Yet by and large, it was the tune and not the words that seemed to catch the American people's fancy. Outside of the large East Coast cities, most who sang or played "Hail to the Chief" believed it to be an American song.

On February 22, 1815, "Hail to the Chief" was made a part of the "Celebration of Peace" held in the Stone Chapel in Boston. This large gathering was the talk of the town and included fireworks, music, and speeches. Officially the Celebration of Peace was held to mark the end of the War of 1812—a conflict that both the Americans and British claimed to have won but that each was more than happy to conclude in a draw. Yet in truth, this was really a party to mark the return of normal life to America.

For the Boston celebration, L. M. Sargent had rewritten "Hail to the Chief" as "Wreaths for the Chieftain." As it was the birthday of George Washington, the song was probably performed as much to honor the memory of the first president as it was to mark the ending of the recent war. Whatever the real reason for the song's rewrite, the crowd loved the new version. Hundreds left humming the tune as they made their way home. The performance struck such a strong chord that overnight sheet-music sales for the various versions of

"Hail to the Chief" doubled. Unable to remember the title, many walked into stores asking for the "Washington Song" or "The President's Anthem."

The popular song remained an American favorite up until the Civil War. By that time, at least a hundred different sets of lyrics had been affixed to "Hail to the Chief." Some of these versions were serious, but in truth, most were humorous and a few were ribald. As a vocal number, it retained very little of the pomp and dignity that it had when performed for President Adams in 1828. Yet when the song was played rather than sung, it seemed to have a character that set it apart from other popular tunes. When arranged for military bands, it sounded almost regal. As a march tune it was powerful, strong, and resolute.

Between the time it was first played for Adams and when it was commonly performed during the Civil War, there is no record of "Hail to the Chief"'s being used for the president's theme song at all formal occasions. There are numerous mentions of the song's being used as a greeting for mayors, congressmen, judges, and even university leaders. A few Native American leaders were even serenaded by "Hail to the Chief" when they made official visits to major United States cities. Because of this, "Hail to the Chief" was played into the ground. It might even have been dismissed as a presidential song if the second wife of President John Tyler had not asked the Marine Band to announce her husband's arrival one night by performing "Hail to the Chief." Another future first lady noted the way the song fit with the office, so Sarah Polk also requested that the marines play the song each time her husband, the next U.S. president, appeared at any formal event. Except for occasional references in newspapers, there is really little mention of the song and the highest office in the land, beyond the requests of those two first ladies. Yet it must have been used for each president after Polk, judging from a later request made by President Chester Arthur.

Arthur did not like "Hail to the Chief." He thought it was undignified and quickly grew so tired of hearing the song that he summoned the United States Marine's bandmaster, John Philip Sousa, to visit the Oval Office. The president ordered Sousa to write a new song to be used when Arthur walked into a room. Sousa answered by composing "Presidential Polonaise." When the public failed to respond with enthusiasm to this presidential musical greeting, Sousa went back to his studio and produced "Semper Fidelis." By the time this work was completed, Arthur was no longer the president. Still, Sousa pushed on. The bandmaster was determined to make "Semper Fidelis" the song of the president. Yet, like "Presidential Polonaise," it failed to catch on. Nevertheless, the Marine Band played it every time the president appeared in Washington; but when President Grover Cleveland was on the road the local bands still used "Hail to the Chief." Eventually even the Marine Band bowed to public pressure and went back to the song taken from the British play. However, Sousa's "Semper Fidelis" was not completely dismissed; it would become the official march of the U.S. Marines.

It is a fact that "Hail to the Chief" has been played for every president since Arthur, and perhaps every chief executive since Adams, yet through two world wars and a long list of "chiefs," it was not officially adopted until 1954. One hundred thirty-nine years after it was played to commemorate the late George Washington's birthday and 126 years after it was first performed to greet a living president, "Hail to the Chief," a tune taken from an English musical, was formally adopted by the Defense Department as the official music of the president of the United States. Some, including President Chester Arthur, might say this was another example of British influence in every facet of American government, but music historians would probably wryly note that the English musical invasion didn't begin in 1964 with the Beatles, but actually started more than two centuries ago with "Hail to the Chief" and "The Star-Spangled Banner."

🎕 17 🎕

I'M A YANKEE DOODLE DANDY

*G*eorge M. Cohan was born on July 3, 1878, but, his father, Jeremiah, a vaudeville trouper, fudged on the date and declared that the newest member of the family clan had actually seen the first light of day on July 4. It was a show business publicity gimmick of which George would have wholeheartedly approved. It now seems clear that the fictitious Independence Day birthday set in motion a career theme that would follow Cohan for the next six decades.

For most of his first twenty-five years of life, George was a member of a touring troupe made up of his older sister, Josephine; his mother, Helen; and his father. The quartet made a solid entertainment team, and by 1900 the Four Cohans were one of the most successful acts in American theater. They functioned so much as a single fluid act that it was almost impossible to think of one without the other three. But though he never wanted the family ensemble to end its run, George realized there would be a time when the quartet would break up and he would have to stand on his own talents. So when he wasn't on stage with the Four Cohans, he worked developing skills that could make the small man a large star in his own right. At twenty-five, he even told a San Francisco newspaper that he felt he was ready to accept that challenge. When his sister left the act and his parents decided to retire soon thereafter, he had no choice. Ready or not, Cohan was a solo act.

In 1904, the young singer-dancer formed a partnership with promoter and businessman Sam Harris. Harris assured Cohan that he could raise the money for a show if George could just compose some solid musical material. When their handshake sealed the deal, most in the New York theater probably didn't think this union would last a year. And except for George himself, no one would have suggested that this team would rock Broadway for a generation.

Cohan never shrunk from a challenge. He thought he could successfully stroll the wooden stage planks in any city in the country. Yet instead of slowly working his way up to the top, he opted to begin at the pinnacle of his profession—the New York stage—where he honestly believed that he would quickly take Broadway by storm. Those who controlled the theaters in the Big Apple were not so sure. After a couple of false starts, a slightly discouraged George was almost broke and desperate for a hit. But while his money was gone and his reputation scarred, his ego remained intact. He still believed in himself above all other things. Surprisingly, he also realized that he needed some help.

In typical Cohan style, the brash young Irish American told his partner that the idea for his next show was all but hatched and ordered Harris out on the streets looking for cash. In truth, Cohan had no ideas for the show. Everything he had penned thus far had

I'm a Yankee Doodle Dandy
A Yankee Doodle, do or die;
A real live nephew of my uncle
    Sam's,
Born on the Fourth of July.
I've got a Yankee Doodle sweet-
    heart,
She's my Yankee Doodle joy.
Yankee Doodle came to London,
Just to ride the ponies,
I am a Yankee Doodle boy.

I'm the kid that's all the candy
I'm a Yankee Doodle Dandy
I'm glad I am
So's Uncle Sam
I'm a real live Yankee Doodle
Made my name and fame and
    boodle
Just like Mister Doodle did,
By riding on a pony
I love to listen to the Dixey
    strain
"I long to see the girl I left behind
    me"
And that ain't a josh
She's a Yankee, by gosh
Oh, say can you see
Anything about a Yankee that's a
    phoney?

I'm a Yankee Doodle Dandy
A Yankee Doodle, do or die;
A real live nephew of my uncle
    Sam's,
Born on the Fourth of July.
I've got a Yankee Doodle sweet-
    heart,
She's my Yankee Doodle joy.
Yankee Doodle came to
    London,
Just to ride the ponies,
I am a Yankee Doodle boy.

Father's name was Hezikiah
Mother's name was Ann Maria
Yanks through and through
Red, white and blue
Father was so Yankee hearted
When the Spanish War was
    started
He slipped on his uniform
And hopped up on a pony
My mother's mother was a Yankee
    true
My father's father was a Yankee too
And that's going some
For the Yankees, by gum
Oh, say can you see
Anything about my pedigree that's
    phoney?

I'm a Yankee Doodle Dandy
A Yankee Doodle, do or die;
A real live nephew of my uncle
  Sam's,
Born on the Fourth of July.

I've got a Yankee Doodle sweetheart,
She's my Yankee Doodle joy.
Yankee Doodle came to London,
Just to ride the ponies,
I am a Yankee Doodle boy.

ended up in the trash can. Nevertheless, Harris managed to obtain some financial backing, and the duo began hiring a cast for the yet unnamed and unwritten vehicle.

As time passed and scores of actors and stage hands joined their troupe, Harris grew worried. Meanwhile the always confident Cohan assured everyone that the show was just an idea away from becoming a reality. Yet it wasn't George's imagination, but a newspaper story that finally inspired that Cohan magic and saved his partner from a nervous breakdown.

George, a rabid baseball fan, was checking out the sports page when he came across an account of an American jockey in England. The more Cohan read, the more fascinated he became with the success of jockey Ted Sloan. Riding to victory after victory, this young American had become the toast of the British Isles. What a story! Cohan thought. And thanks to the newspaper and the jockey, the writer had an idea for a show. With Sloan in mind, George picked up pen and paper and finally went to work on his newest play. This would mark the first time Cohan would use something other than one of his family's old vaudeville routines as inspiration for a musical. Using London as the principal setting, he penned a piece about a jockey, a fixed race, and redemption. He managed to work in a Cohan staple as well, a large dose of good old American flag waving.

With material in hand and Cohan as the star, the troupe went to work learning the lines, dance steps, and music to *Little Johnny Jones*. It took sixteen-hour days and weeks of work, but finally the play was ready to open. Rather than risking everything with a New York premiere, Cohan and Harris made their debut in Hartford, Connecticut. With less than fifty dollars between them, the anxious team looked to the opening-night crowd for their reviews. When the audience leaped to their feet cheering during the song "I'm a Yankee Doodle Dandy," the men felt assured they had a hit play.

"Yankee Doodle" had always been the alter ego of George Cohan. His father had called him the "Yankee Doodle Baby" and later the "Yankee Doodle Boy." George had often even billed himself as the "Yankee Doodle Comedian." Yet though the writer Cohan might not have realized it when he penned "Yankee Doodle Dandy," the performer Cohan knew the song was magic when he watched the Hartford crowd respond to his singing it. After the show, scores of fans told George that it was the first number that anyone could remember that was both humorous and patriotic. Best of all, unlike many songs put into plays of the period, it was really significant to the musical's plot. Yet what no one on that first evening could have realized was that "Yankee Doodle Dandy" would have a life beyond *Little Johnny Jones*. This number would come to represent George M. Cohan and every other person who showed unbridled pride in the United States.

John Philip Sousa had opened up the nation to the strains of patriotic music more than a decade before "Yankee Doodle Dandy" had been written. With this in mind, Cohan had to have believed a number like "I'm a Yankee Doodle Dandy" would strike a chord with American audiences. After all, over the past twenty years a love-of-country fever had swept the country. Cohan was well aware that for years parades, band concerts, and other musicals had been embracing patriotism. The Spanish-American War and the Theodore Roosevelt presidency had pushed this patriotic fever to an even higher pitch. It showed no signs of diminishing either. American flags and red, white, and blue bunting were everywhere, and patriotic songs were ruling the song charts of the period. Living in this environment must have convinced the writer to pull out every patriotic stop from his arsenal of song ideas when working on *Little Johnny Jones*. Yet while "Yankee Doodle Dandy" tied in with what was important to most Americans at the time, it was more than just a song that capitalized on the writer's sense of what would sell. The number also reflected who George M. Cohan really was.

Those who knew Cohan well realized that "Yankee Doodle Dandy" was largely an autobiographical ode, less about the jockey who had inspired the play and more about George M. Cohan himself. The song also represented an important element of Cohan's success. Since the moment of his father's claiming July 4 as George's birthday, the family had traded on the Stars and Stripes and all things red, white, and blue in almost every show they had ever performed. George grew up a flag-waver and really did have a special love for his country. Thus, as he played and sang "Yankee Doodle Dandy" in the voice of a brash and cocky American jockey, it was really George M. playing George M. So when audiences responded strongly to the song, in Cohan's mind they were also approving of him as well.

Though it was a big hit in Hartford, Cohan's newest play did not work well during its initial release on Broadway at the Liberty Theater. Reviewers were lukewarm, and the audiences were little more than polite. *Little Johnny Jones* quickly closed in New York, but Cohan and Harris had too much money invested in the production to give up. They gathered up the cast, boarded a train, and took the musical on the road. So for an entire year the troupe worked the American heartland, appearing in city after city, and night after night, large crowds flocked to catch the grand production. In those months Cohan reworked and fine-tuned his show. Over time he eliminated every weakness, every flaw, and every low point. He then polished the musical and comedy bits until they shone. By the end of the road run it was a much different show than it had been when it had closed on Broadway. So it was hardly surprising that when *Little Johnny Jones* did return to New York, the response was far different. The second time around proved to be a charm, thanks to the show's now clean flow and to its two inspired songs, "Give My Regards to Broadway" and "I'm a Yankee Doodle Dandy."

"I'm a Yankee Doodle Dandy" was still being sung long after *Little Johnny Jones* had closed and Cohan and Harris had moved on to other hit shows. It became a national favorite during the First World War and remained a staple of school plays and small-town theater productions throughout the twenties and thirties. Yet it would take a second global war and a Hollywood movie to establish this song as one of the most endearing and beloved numbers in American history.

George M. Cohan had retired by the time rumors of war crackled through newspapers and radio news reports in 1941. Still, the great patriot, like so many others, realized that given time American troops would again be waging battles overseas. As he dabbled with writing and spoke with friends about the state of the world, the Warner Brothers studio approached the man and asked if he would allow them to film a musical biography of his life. At first he emphatically said no. Cohan had enjoyed living his life, but he didn't want to relive it by watching it on screen. Yet the more he considered the concept, the more the "Prince of Broadway" became convinced that this was another and perhaps final chance at having a big hit Cohan show. Ultimately he not only gave his consent, he also helped write the script.

Jimmy Cagney was signed to play Cohan; the great Walter Huston was brought in as the father; Cagney's own sister, Jeannie, was given the part of Josephine; Rosemary DeCamp portrayed George's mother; and the darling of the Warner's set at the time, seventeen-year-old Joan Leslie, won the role of the songwriter's beloved wife, Agnes Mary. Yet as great as were the costars' performances, it was really all Cagney's show. This was fitting because in every one of Cohan's own musicals and plays, it had always been George M.'s show as well.

Besides the almost perfect casting, the studio also showed great wisdom when it opted to title the epic *Yankee Doodle Dandy*. After all, this song really did reflect the way Cohan viewed himself and the way the world viewed Cohan. In that number, as well as in the entire two hours and six minutes of the movie, the Cohan legend and fact blended together so well that it was hard to tell one from the other. So naturally, while the movie was a four-star smash, it was less about the songwriter's life than it was about his music and his time spent on stage.

Cohan went to see *Yankee Doodle Dandy* realizing that his days were limited. Though only a few close friends and family knew it, cancer was eating up his body from the inside out. Yet as he watched his film biography, he seemed to understand that the music that represented so much of his life and work would not pass away when he did. It would live on, inspiring new generations of his countrymen, reminding them what it meant to be called an American.

There is a line in *Little Johnny Jones* when a confused Englishman asks Jones, "What makes Americans so proud?"

Without missing a beat Jones replies, "Other countries." This wasn't just a character spewing out a meaningless line from a script; it was the real Yankee Doodle Dandy, aka George M. Cohan, saying what he really believed.

On November 4, 1942, George M. Cohan lay dying. A close theater friend leaned over and whispered to the Broadway showman, "You've had quite a life, George." Cohan opened his eyes, smiled, and replied, "No complaints, kid. No complaints."

To the end, the legendary showman remained the essence of his creation. George M. Cohan didn't just pen the song; he was "Yankee Doodle Dandy."

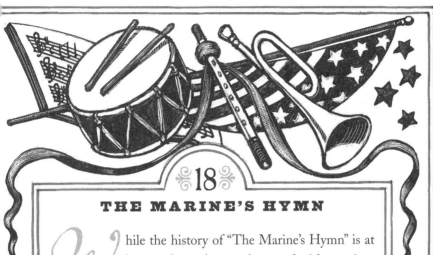

18

THE MARINE'S HYMN

hile the history of "The Marine's Hymn" is at best unclear, what can be stated with certainty is that this well-known song is the oldest of the United States service anthems. At the least, the hymn dates to the days after the Civil War, and if legend is correct, the song's origins might even go back as far as 1847. Though a host of different marines, including the legendary John Philip Sousa, have tried on several occasions to uncover the mysterious roots of "The Marine's Hymn," even these tough men and women have found that this is one battle they cannot win. This vibrant song has managed to hang on to the secrets of its birth.

A German named Jacques Offenbach figures prominently in the history of "The Marine's Hymn." Though he is often called a French composer, Offenbach was actually born in Cologne on June 20, 1819. He would move to France when he entered the Paris Conservatoire at the age of nineteen. Upon graduation from the prestigious school, he was given a spot as a cellist at the Opera Comique. In 1847, Offenbach became conductor of the Theatre Francais and began to compose operas that became popular in both Europe and the United States.

In 1859, Offenbach wrote a new two-act opera called *Geneviéve de Brabant.* The production was so successful that the composer expanded it to three acts just after Christmas in 1867. In the revised version of the opera, the writer inserted a duet entitled "Couplets des hommes d'armes." This song contains many of the musical elements that were used in "The Marine's Hymn." While the tune does vary somewhat from the one employed in the now famous United States service number, it is assumed by many that it was the German who lived in France who gave the marines the melody for their official song. Most likely this marriage of American words and French music happened after October 22, 1868, for it was on that date that the opera made its U.S. debut in New York City. If Offenbach was the author of the tune, then the following story as to how "The Marine's Hymn"'s original lyrics came into existence would seem to be little more than a fable.

In 1805, during a conflict with the Barbary pirates, Lieutenant P. N. O'Bannon and a small force of marines participated in the capture of Derna, in present-day Libya. This was the first time that Americans had ever raised their flag over any fortress in the Old World. To mark the historic event, the marines inscribed on their banner the location of the action, "To the Shores of Tripoli." These words would remain on their battle flag for the next forty-two years.

In 1847, the marines were again called upon to capture a foreign stronghold. During the war with Mexico, an impressive force of marines easily defeated the Mexican forces, occupied Mexico City, and took over the famed Castle of Chapultepec. The castle was

From the Halls of Montezuma
  To the shores of Tripoli;
We fight our country's battles
  On the land as on the sea;
First to fight for right and freedom
  And to keep our honor clean;
We are proud to claim the title
  Of United States Marine.

Our flag's unfurl'd to ev'ry breeze
  From dawn to setting sun;
We have fought in ev'ry clime and
    place
  Where we could take a gun;
In the snow of far off Northern
  lands

And in sunny tropic scenes;
You will find us always on the
    job—
  The United States Marines.

Here's health to you and to our
    Corps
  Which we are proud to serve;
In many a strife we've fought for
    life
  And never lost our nerve;
If the Army and the Navy
  Ever look on Heaven's scenes;
They will find the streets are
    guarded
  By United States Marines.

known locally as "the Halls of Montezumas," and raising the American flag over this site made headlines across the United States. Because of the honor this action brought to the marines, the words on their banner were then changed to read "From the Shores of Tripoli to the Halls of the Montezuma." While this addition might well have triggered the "The Marine's Hymn"'s noble beginnings, it also warned the world that the U.S. Marines would go anywhere in the world to defend American interests.

Supposedly, during this occupation of Mexico, inspired by the action he had just witnessed, an anonymous leatherneck sat down at his post, picked up pencil and paper, and tried to put into words what he had just witnessed. Legend claims that this soldier was so overwhelmed by the pride he felt in serving his country as a marine that he was able to quickly write a poem that would become the first verse of "The Marine's Hymn." Some military historians also claim that this song was sung by the forces in Mexico and brought back to the United States at the end of the occupation.

If the song was written in Mexico in 1847, then it would fit that the writer would switch the order of the historical events. To him the victory in Mexico would have seemed more important than the battle in Tripoli. Thus it was the taking of the Halls of Montezuma that kicked off the anthem's first line. The rest of that initial stanza would also seem to fit well with the thoughts of a young man who had survived a battle and was proud that his unit had performed so well. The legend of this birth of "The Marine's Hymn" can also gain a degree of credibility because the elementary use of words fits a common soldier and not an educated musician, and because the initial verse of the old song begins with action in Mexico, indicating a pre–Civil War viewpoint and that the man was familiar with only the marines' history through the Mexican War. So it would seem that a solid claim could be made that at least a part of the song was written in Mexico. Yet if that is the case, then how could the words and meter fit so perfectly with the music written by Offenbach in his opera more than two decades later? Some music historians claim that the marines did not borrow from Offenbach; rather, the composer borrowed from the Spanish.

At about the same time that the marines occupied Mexico, Spanish folk songs were popular in the capital city. There was one popular guitar piece whose tune seemed to mirror the Offenbach duet "Couplets des hommes d'armes." This folk song was known in both Spain and France. If the opera composer was inspired by a Spanish folk song that was popular more than twenty years before he composed *Geneviéve de Brabant,* then this same song could have been used by the nameless American who wrote the first verse of "The Marine's Hymn." If that was the case, then it would lend validity to "The Marine's Hymn" 's being born in Mexico, thus making it the only U.S. service song to originate in a foreign country.

Beginning in the days after the Civil War, other unknown men wrote more verses to "The Marine's Hymn." For a while, every major battle inspired another addition. In time there were so many different stanzas in the song that no one knew all the words.

On June 23, 1918, while reporting on the exploits of the marines in World War I, the *Kansas City Journal* first published some of the song's lyrics. "The Marine's Hymn" was spotlighted by the paper because of reports from Europe that the marines were singing the anthem as they charged enemy lines. The singing of this song in heated battles had so inspired the French and British troopers that they too had learned the words and joined the Americans as they sang the hymn. Thanks to the story by the *Kansas City Journal,* a feature that was picked up by other newspapers around the country, "The Marine's Hymn" suddenly became larger than life. After decades of being the "unofficial song of the marines," now everyone was either talking about "The Marine's Hymn" or singing it.

On August 1, 1918, the United States Marine Corps printed both the words and the music and released "The Marine's Hymn" to the public for the very first time. Bands throughout the country then began to play it regularly and it quickly became as well known as the popular songs of the era. Yet it would be another decade before the commandant of the Marine Corps authorized "The Marine's Hymn" as the official song of America's oldest service branch. From that point on, the Marine Band, a proud unit that could trace its roots back to 1798, played it at every appearance.

The song remained as it was first printed until World War II. Gunnery Sergeant H. L. Tallman, who had participated in scores of combat missions with the Marine Corps Aviation Force on the western front during World War I, read through the words and decided that the lyrics were dated. In his mind "The Marine's Hymn" did not tell the full story. At a meeting of the First Marine Aviation Force Veterans Association in Cincinnati, Ohio, Tallman proposed a small change in the song's lyrics in order to include all the men who were then playing a vital role in defending their country. The commandant of the Marine Corps agreed and during the midst of World War II approved the only change that has been made to the hymn since it was adopted. "On the land as on the sea" became "In the air, on land, and sea."

Whether French or Spanish in origin, it would seem to be appropriate that the music for "The Marine's Hymn" was born on foreign shores, because the United States Marines have been fighting all around the globe for the cause of freedom and liberty since the inception of the nation. It also seems appropriate that the men who wrote the lyrics to this popular and beloved song are unknown, because it has long been the nameless, faceless, and selfless marines who have brought such great honor to this renowned branch of the military. As a proud symbol of all the men and women who have earned the title "the few and the brave," "The Marine's Hymn" proudly proclaims the unique character and history of the marines and has taken its place as one of the world's best-known and most respected military songs.

19

MY COUNTRY 'TIS OF THEE (AMERICA)

The United States of America was just beginning its great experiment in democracy when Samuel Francis Smith was born in Newton Centre, Massachusetts, in 1808. A bright child with a creative mind, he was fortunate enough to be a part of a family that had the resources to ensure for the child a quality education. While still a teen, Smith left home to continue his studies at Harvard. During his time at the prestigious college, one of his classmates, Oliver Wendell Holmes, wrote a whimsical poem about the student from Newton Centre:

> And there's a fine youngster of excellent pith,
> Fate tried to conceal him by naming him Smith.

Little did the soon to be lionized Holmes or anyone else realize that Smith's creativity would bring him recognition more quickly than it would come to any of the other men who made up the Harvard class of 1829. It can even be argued that Smith's work would also make a more lasting impact than even that of the future Supreme Court justice.

After obtaining a degree from Harvard, Smith studied theology at Andover Seminary. It was there, in 1832, that a research assignment would trigger inspiration that is still being felt today.

A close friend of Smith's, William Woolbridge, had just returned from Germany. His tour of the old country, especially the visits to ancient cathedrals, had deeply moved Woolbridge. He told Smith that though he didn't know much of the language, the music he heard from the German choirs had lifted his soul to new heights. The American tourist had even picked up songbooks while on the tour, bringing them back to America in hopes of having some of the songs translated for use at the seminary and in local churches. Upon his return, Woolbridge had given these books to one of New England's greatest vocalists, Lowell Mason. While interested in the reasons his friend had been so moved by German hymns and in the stories about the recent trip, at that moment Mason could not foresee how one tune in the books that Woolbridge had brought back would touch him and millions of others.

Though he had accepted the hymnals, Lowell Mason did not read German. He thumbed through the volumes but found them to be of little use. Rather than keeping the books, he sought out Samuel Smith. Smith, who was at least a bit familiar with the German language, seemed a better choice to review the material. If the student found anything that was deemed worthy of using, Mason asked that the lyrics be translated and brought back to him. Mason probably never expected that Smith would find even one worthy song in the

My country 'tis of thee,
Sweet land of liberty,
Of thee I sing.
Land where my fathers died!
Land of the Pilgrim's pride!
From every mountain side,
Let freedom ring!

My native country, thee,
Land of the noble free,
Thy name I love.
I love thy rocks and rills,
Thy woods and templed hills;
My heart with rapture fills
Like that above.

Let music swell the breeze,
And ring from all the trees
Sweet freedom's song.
Let mortal tongues awake;
Let all that breathe partake;
Let rocks their silence break,
The sound prolong.

Our father's God, to Thee,
Author of liberty,
To Thee we sing.
Long may our land be bright
With freedom's holy light;
Protect us by Thy might,
Great God, our King!

songbooks. Ultimately, the singer didn't even care enough to check on the student's progress.

In truth, Smith was not very interested in the German songs either. This style of music did not excite him. At this time America was alive with its own folk music, and most people were trying to rid themselves of the old European songs in favor of homegrown tunes. So Smith naturally set the books aside and worked on other things. He finally got to them on a cold February day. With the north wind howling, the skies dark, and only the hymnals on his study table, the student was faced with the prospects of either going out into that frigid gray afternoon or finally tackling Mason's request. Picking the lesser of two evils, Smith forced himself to sit down, picked up the books, and began to leaf through them.

As he studied the music to the first few songs, he couldn't figure out why Woolbridge had been so moved. As a matter of fact, for several minutes nothing in that first book hit Smith as being either interesting or exciting. Then a tune he had never heard leaped from the page. It was simple and possessed a very unchallenging range and straightforward melody. In this particular book, the verses were written not in between the musical staffs as they are today, but at the bottom of each page. After humming the melody several times, Smith glanced down and read the lyrics.

Smith quickly realized that this was not a typical Christian hymn. What he had just uncovered had been written to salute and ask blessings for the German rulers. Strange, he thought, this song was not typical of a national anthem; it lacked the pomp and circumstance that usually accompanied salutes to a king or queen. The student then quickly read back over the lyrics of the first verse, translating them into English.

God save our gracious King,
Long live our noble King,
God save the King!
Send her victorious,
Happy and Glorious,
Long to reign over us;

Smith hummed through the melody a few more times to imprint it into his mind, then again reviewed the original words. Realizing that the task of going through the old songs had produced some fruit, he felt a need to do something. Yet as much as he liked the tune, he knew that a direct translation of the words would not serve Mason's or Woolbridge's needs.

"When I came across the air 'God Save the King,'" Smith later told his family, "I liked the music. I glanced at the German words at the foot of the page. Under the inspiration of the moment I went to work and in half an hour 'America' was the result. It was written on a scrap of paper I picked up from the table, and the hymn of today is substantially as it was written on that day."

When finished, Smith braved the cold wind and shared his song with Mason and Woolbridge. Over the next few days the new work was also sung and played for seminary professors and students. Everyone agreed that the young man had created something special. Maybe of more importance, most thought it did not sound the least bit German. Rather, the melody seemed more like the folk music that was being sung at that time in the United States. After the song was arranged for multipart harmonies, it was decided that Smith's "America" would make a wonderful number for a choir. Plans were set in motion, and on July 4, 1832, at the Park Street Church in

Boston, "America" made its debut. The voices of five hundred children brought the new hymn to life on that Independence Day, or as it was usually called then, Declaration Day.

Smith, Woolbridge, and Mason did not imagine that anyone in the crowd would recognize the tune that had been found in the old hymnal. Yet as the crowd listened, many found the melody very familiar. Those with an English background immediately realized that this new American patriotic ode was being sung to the tune of the British national anthem, "God Save the King." As there was still a deep rift between many Americans and the English, especially in Boston, it was immediately suggested that the inspired words found in "America" might be better suited for a melody that came from somewhere other than Great Britain.

Smith had evidently never heard "God Save the King." He did not know that he had set his "America" to a tune that was known throughout the British Empire. He also did not realize that this melody had been used for a number of other early American patriotic songs, including "God Save the President" and "God Save George Washington." At the turn of the century this tune had even been combined with a Fourth of July poem called "Come All Ye Sons of Song." Smith, who just minutes before had seemed like a genius and a hero, now faced a number of anti-British critics and had to deflect a rash of criticism for matching his lyrics to the song used to hail an old foe's ruler. Yet even as many joined this chorus, the student was not moved to change his song.

To make a point, Smith retrieved the German book that had supplied the song and pointed out that "God Bless Saxony" was not English at all. This book seemed to prove that the tune was actually German in origin. This news came as a shock to many not only in

America, but across the seas as well. The English had long argued that Henry Carey had written the music in 1715. No self-respecting Englishman believed this could be true, they thought of the song as purely British.

Smith did not bother tracing the song any further back than the old hymnal, but others did. The *New York Sun*'s research uncovered that the tune had first surfaced in America as "Whitefield's Tune" and had then been matched with another set of lyrics. This same melody also existed in Prussia, where it was also used as that nation's national anthem, as well as Spain, Norway, and Finland. The *Sun* even declared that there was evidence to support the theory that the tune had been sung in Asia and that the Huns had brought it back to Europe after fighting a war there. So where did it really originate? Who really wrote it? In truth, no one can accurately say. Meanwhile, in England, all claims of origin were dismissed except those that gave full credit to the British song scribe Carey. In Germany, music historians claimed that Germans had been singing it for hundreds of years and that no other country could or should declare it as its own.

"America" quickly became a New England favorite. By the 1850s it was being used in many hymnals, but outside of its use for Independence or Declaration Day church services, the song was not widely sung throughout the United States until the Civil War. It was during this traumatic time that Americans really began to use and lean on patriotic symbols and songs. On the day the flag was shot down at Fort Sumter, "America" was sung in Washington as if these words would mend the now broken nation. As a symbol of solidarity and strength, "America" continued to be sung in the North at flag raisings, funerals, church services, and government meetings throughout the remainder of the war. When the Union was preserved, "America" was unofficially adopted as the nation's anthem.

Smith, who not only pastored several New England churches but traveled all across the globe on missionary journeys, seemed to find his song wherever Americans gathered. "I heard it on the Atlantic Ocean," he wrote during his later years, "on the Baltic Sea and on the Mediterranean, in London, in Liverpool, Stockholm, Copenhagen, Paris, Rome, Naples, in the baths at Pompeii, in Athens, Calcutta and Rangoon. On the earth I have heard it on Pikes Peak, and under the earth at the caverns at Manitou, Colorado, where it was played on stalactites. It has been sung on battlefields, on many a march, in hospitals and on days of great rejoicing and on days that were dark and uncertain." The fact that his thirty-minute effort had come to mean so much to so many must have pleased the writer a great deal.

There can be little doubt that for the last forty years of the nineteenth century, "America" was the most beloved song in the nation. It meant so much to those in the United States that this hymn was treated as if it were sacred, and Samuel Smith almost became as much the symbol of liberty as did his words. In his later years, people would travel for days just to meet and shake the hand of the man who had penned "America." In 1895, the pope even requested a copy of "America" written in the Baptist minister's own hand. This manuscript still rests in the Vatican Library.

In 1899, three years after Smith had died, Col. Nicholas Smith (no relation) wrote of "America," "It is recognized the world over as a great national hymn—beautifully simple in its poetry, rich in its patriotic sentiment, and vigorous enough to reflect the ennobling spirit of true American liberty." In his book *Stories of Great National*

Songs, Col. Smith summed up "America"'s true power like this: "The song is simplicity itself, and yet it is a curious fact that others more gifted in poetic faculty, and of greater minds than Dr. Smith, have tried their best to make a song which would be truly a national anthem, but no one except this plain, kindly and noble-hearted Baptist clergyman has come within a thousand miles of success."

The reason "America" did not become the official national anthem is probably rooted in the fact that the English had already claimed the tune as their patriotic standard. Most Americans didn't want the world to think that they could not come up with an original national song. Ironically, when in 1931, the United States did finally choose a song as the country's official anthem, it was a set of American lyrics matched to a tune that really did originate in Great Britain. Yet even though "America" lost out to "The Star-Spangled Banner," the song's impact on the country cannot be diminished. It has probably been sung in more churches and schools, and on more battlefields than any other song in American history.

Seven decades after Samuel Smith died, another Baptist preacher would use "America" as inspiration. This time it was Dr. Martin Luther King Jr. In the midst of his famous "I Have a Dream" speech, King echoed Smith's words and then added to them.

> *This will be the day when all of God's children will be able to sing with a new meaning, 'My country, 'tis of thee, sweet land of liberty, of thee I sing. Land where my fathers died, land of the pilgrim's pride, from every mountainside, let freedom ring.'*
>
> *And if America is to be a great nation this must become true. So let freedom ring from the prodigious hilltops of New Hamp-*

shire. Let freedom ring from the mighty mountains of New York. Let freedom ring from the heightening Alleghenies of Pennsylvania! . . .

From every mountainside, let freedom ring.

It might have started as an assignment to uncover a new hymn for use in a New England seminary, yet "America" has come to mean so much more. "My Country 'Tis of Thee" represents the ideals of liberty and freedom as well as any song ever written. Samuel Smith probably realized that the day he first penned it. Abraham Lincoln knew this when he asked a nation to sing this song as he and millions of others fought to preserve the Union. Martin Luther King Jr. realized it when he prepared for the most important speech of his life.

Smith's old classmate, the chief justice of the Supreme Court Oliver Wendell Holmes, also well knew the power of the song. A year before his death, Holmes wrote, "Now, there's Smith. His name will be honored by every school child in the land when I have been forgotten a hundred years. He wrote 'My Country 'Tis of Thee.' If he had said, 'Our Country,' the hymn would not have been immortal, but that 'My' was a masterstroke. Every one who sings the hymn at once feels a personal ownership in this native land. The hymn will last as long as the country."

⟨20⟩

OVER THERE

*O*n April 6, 1917, President Woodrow Wilson signed a declaration of war against Germany. It was a Friday and George M. Cohan took the news as most Americans did—he was not very worried. The American attitude of the day was that our men were simply better, smarter, braver, and stronger than any other men on earth. We had tamed the great western frontier; we were building huge industrial facilities. The ideas of inventors and industrialists from our nation were revolutionizing the world, so, most believed, who could possibly challenge an American at anything? It was a fact of the time that most Americans really believed that they were the greatest men and women on earth. So naturally millions honestly felt that American soldiers would whip the German armies in a matter of weeks.

On the New York City and Long Island streets that Cohan called home, talk of the war was everywhere that spring day. The generally accepted idea was that "when we get over there, it will all be over in weeks." This concept was one that the composer must have heard a dozen times on April 6 alone. That night he began to play with those words and mold them into a song. He later told his friends that he wrote the chorus in minutes and completed the whole number in a half an hour. Knowing how fast Cohan worked, that is not doubted. What is debated to this day is if the song was written in New York City at his office or theater, or at his home at Great Neck. The Cohan family would claim that it was written at home. Others believe that "Over There" was hatched in Cohan's mind as he drove to his office on April 7 and that the songwriter scribbled out the lyrics as soon as he arrived at his office and finished the music at his theater later that day. The one thing that seems sure is that it was probably the easiest song the tunesmith had ever produced. It just flowed out of his mind like water from a tap. When he finished, he didn't have to rework any of the lyrics or the tune.

On Sunday morning, April 8, Cohan called all his children together to listen to his newest work. This wasn't a request, it was an order. To set the mood, the master showman put a tin pan on his head and carried a broom in his hands. He was playing soldier. He sang, he marched, he danced, and he laughed. He was so convincing that his children really believed he was going to join the military. Cohan's kids cried in fear of their father going to war until he informed them that "Over There" was just a song. At this point, based on his family's response, the composer felt he had a winner.

Cohan would later tell his friends that "Over There" was really just a bugle call. To him it was nothing more than a singing version of reveille. Those who listened carefully to the chorus could imagine a bugle too. Yet the master composer would soon discover that it was to mean much more to most Americans than just a wake-up tune.

Johnnie, get your gun,
Get your gun, get your gun,
Take it on the run,
On the run, on the run.
Hear them calling, you and me,
Every son of liberty.
Hurry right away,
No delay, no delay,
Make your daddy glad
To have had such a lad.
Tell your sweetheart not to pine.
To be proud her boy's in line.

Chorus:
Over there, over there,
Send the word, send the word over
    there—
That the Yanks are coming,
The Yanks are coming,
The drums rum-tumming
Ev'rywhere.

So prepare, say a pray'r,
Send the word, send the word to
    beware.
We'll be over, we're coming
    over,
And we won't come back till it's
    over
Over there.

Johnnie, get your gun,
Get your gun, get your gun,
Johnnie show the Hun
Who's a son of a gun.
Hoist the flag and let her fly,
Yankee Doodle do or die.
Pack your little kit,
Show your grit, do your bit.
Yankee Doodle fill the ranks,
From the towns and the tanks.
Make your mother proud of you,
And the old Red, White and Blue.

Nora Bayes was the first of many to record "Over There." In 1917 alone seven different recording artists would place the song on the charts. Besides Bayes, the American Quartet, the Peerless Quartet, and Enrico Caruso all hit number 1 with "Over There." Prince's Orchestra and Billy Murray also put the tune into the Top 10 on the national playlists. In less than two months, the latest Cohan hit would sell more than a million records. Yet it was more than just a record—it was the song on everyone's lips from border to border and coast to coast. This was proven time and time again when everywhere the composer traveled he found himself being serenaded by his newest hit. Cohan's singing bugle call would become the most popular song of the war years, easily topping Irving Berlin's "Oh How I Hate to Get Up in the Morning," a fact that must have brought a great deal of satisfaction to the master of Broadway.

By 1917, George M. Cohan was on top of his game. He was the toast of not just New York and the Broadway district, but all of America and most of the world. Before he was finished, he would write forty plays and have a hand in four times that many productions. He would make more than a thousand appearances as an actor on Broadway alone. He would also pen almost five hundred songs. This son of vaudeville entertainers might have called himself just a "song and dance man," but beginning with his 1905 Broadway hit *Little Johnny Jones,* he was the heart of American theater and music for almost four decades.

"Over There" captured the spirit of Americans as perfectly as any song ever had. Few in the overly optimistic United States of 1917 knew what war really was like. The Civil War and all its death and destruction were a very distant memory. Because they just didn't recall the real cost of battle or the horrors of war, many Americans of this time thought that this country was indestructible. This American sense of invincibility caught on in Europe as well, transported by troops singing Cohan's "Over There" as they landed in Britain and France.

It was natural that after seeing American troops boldly singing this song as they swaggered off their troopships, the English and French also adopted "Over There" as a song of salvation. The people of these nations saw the Americans as the trump card they needed to chase the Germans back to Berlin. Heaven knows the Allies needed such a boost too. The war had been brutal and costly. Many families had lost their loved ones and a generation of young men were being killed on a slow day-by-day, week-by-week basis. Hope was in short supply, so the Yanks singing "Over There" was like a breath of spring air. Newspapers covering the war even called the Cohan tune the Allies' "Victory Hymn."

What the American troops, as well as the British and French, would quickly discover was that the enemy didn't buy into the optimism that the Yanks brought with them. The Germans knew that bullets and gas would kill those from New York and Los Angeles, and all points in between, as easily as it had men from London and Paris. Tens of thousands of innocent Americans would soon discover that fact as well. Still, they didn't run, and the Yanks did stay until it was over, over there.

"Over There" was put away at the end of the war, supposedly never to be needed again. The war to end all wars was finished, and the world was theoretically safe forever. Yet just as the Americans' innocent attitude about the price of war was proven wrong in 1917 and 1918, so was the idea that this first victory in the war in Europe had ended war forever on the planet. By the late 1930s, the Germans had again brought destruction to our former allies. As the rumors of war hovered in the air, Americans were no longer as cocky as they had been a generation earlier. Millions now knew the real cost of war firsthand and didn't want to have to go to battle again.

By 1936, Cohan had lived long enough to go from being a bit player in vaudeville to being hailed as the Prince of the American Theater. Congress and a president Cohan often spoofed voted to award the Toast of the Great White Way a Congressional Medal of Honor. This was not the same award given to military men for valor, but a special one designated just for Cohan as a way of saying thanks for inspiring Americans through his music. Ironically, Cohan did not rush to the White House to pick up that medal. He really didn't want it at all.

Though Cohan's large ego was well known, he didn't like awards. He had been offered countless degrees, keys to cities, special titles, and other honors, and he either turned most of them down or didn't show up when they were handed out. Even the man's love for America didn't move him to change his principles in 1936. So for four years his medal sat waiting for him at 1600 Pennsylvania Avenue.

In 1940, with war looming, the Prince of Broadway finally put aside his own reservations about honors and awards and paid a visit to President Franklin Roosevelt. He later wrote down the events of that meeting, noting that as he visited with FDR he had observed, "Where else in the world could a plain guy like me sit down and talk things over with the head man?" According to Cohan, the president replied, "Well now, you know, Mr. Cohan, that's as good a definition of America as I've ever heard."

On December 7, 1941, the United States could no longer pretend that the wars in Europe and Asia really were not a threat to its shores. After the attack on Pearl Harbor, and after President Roosevelt's address to Congress and the nation, George M. Cohan turned on his radio and once again listened to his optimistic musical call to arms. The country's attitude was not as cocky as it had been a generation before. There were too many recent memories of death and injury to take the outcome of this Second World War for granted. Even the flag-waving grand old songmaster was a bit fearful of the battles that lay ahead.

A few months after the United States entered the war, Warner Brothers released a film version of Cohan's life, *Yankee Doodle Dandy*. As the aging Broadway performer watched Jimmy Cagney portray him on the silver screen, Cohan told his family, "They got it right." His daughter Georgette later wryly observed, "That was the life that Dad would have liked to have lived."

George M. Cohan was fighting cancer when Americans flocked to see the movie about him. As he fought his private battle, thanks to both the movie and the war, he again heard choirs singing his classic call to arms.

By the late summer of 1942, Cohan was all but housebound. Intestinal cancer had stolen the energy from his legs and heart. Yet one late-summer evening, the composer resolved to be the old George M. one more time. Resolutely he strolled into his living room and beckoned his nurse. "We are going down to Broadway," he declared. A few minutes later they were in the car passing along sidewalks filled with men and women trying to forget about a brutal war being fought on two fronts. After driving by many of his past haunts, Cohan stopped at his old theater. He then went to Union Square, where he had once worked with his parents and sister. Finally he drove back to the Hollywood Theatre. There he parked his car. Cohan and his nurse stopped at the ticket office, bought two tickets, and found seats in the back row. For several minutes they watched the movie version of his life. As Cagney and a group of marching soldiers began to sing "Over There," Cohan nodded and got up. Walking out into the night air, he looked around, smiled, and shook his head as if saying good-bye. Though no one except his nurse had noticed, the master had given his "regards to Broadway" for the very last time.

Cohan died on November 5. His last words were "look after Agnes," the woman he had married more than thirty years before. The sixty-four-year-old composer's funeral was attended by everyone from movie and stage stars to military brass to common folk. In one of the service's most moving moments, the organist played a very slow version of "Over There." This time the song seemed to serve as a warning to heaven and Saint Peter that a very stubborn and proud Yank was coming to pay a call.

"Over There" didn't seem to fit the national mood during the wars in Korea and Vietnam, and it was not played much during that time. Yet after the events of September 11, 2001, a united America once again responded as one nation to a challenge to make things right "Over There," and Cohan's great song, along with his "You're a Grand Old Flag," were in style again.

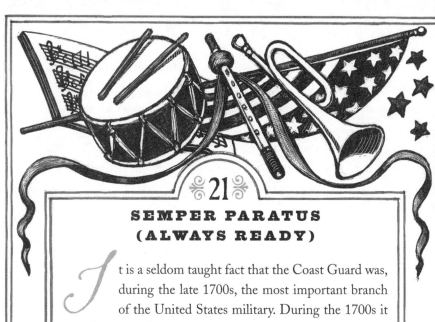

21

SEMPER PARATUS
(ALWAYS READY)

t is a seldom taught fact that the Coast Guard was, during the late 1700s, the most important branch of the United States military. During the 1700s it was the Coast Guard that not only protected the American coastline against enemies, which included pirates, but also operated as the nation's seagoing police force, stemming the business of smuggling. In the days before income tax, import duties kept the new nation afloat, so catching goods before they were illegally brought into the country was essential. Without the activities of the Coast Guard, it is doubtful that the United States could have paid its bills during this period.

In spite of its vital importance to the fledgling nation, for almost a century the Coast Guard was a ragtag fleet. Those who served in this loosely defined and little-coordinated branch of the service were literally men for hire. It was only after the Civil War that this military branch would finally become a tightly controlled and highly trained group of fighting men. It was also during this time that the organization's motto, "semper paratus," which means "always ready," was unofficially adopted. And it would not be until the twentieth century that someone finally put music to that motto in a song that really told the true story of the United States Coast Guard and its underappreciated fighting force.

World War I veteran, the first American to spot a German U-boat off the United States coast, an officer since 1891—the "Old Man," as many in his crew called him, was a living picture of what the Coast Guard had grown into. Incredibly loyal, diligent, and always focused on his duties, the captain probably knew more about this often overlooked service branch than anyone in uniform.

Van Boskerck's commands had taken him all over the world, from the Bering Sea and Arctic Ocean to the Gulf Coast and great spans of the Pacific. He had been baked by tropical suns and frozen by arctic winds, and had sailed into the teeth of hurricanes. He had fired at America's enemies, rescued countless fishermen, and stopped smugglers of all kinds. He was so much a sailor that many thought he had salt flowing in his veins and owned only military-issued clothing. It was therefore hardly surprising that the "Old Man" would be the first to attempt to put his extraordinary Coast Guard experiences on paper.

Van Boskerck had witnessed heroism for more than three decades and had seen men lose their lives, quietly serving their nation. He had observed triumphs and tragedies. So there can be little doubt that the "Semper Paratus" poem he composed that day was based on his own experiences. As his own military career wound down, as his days in the service were now numbered, Van Boskerck must have also felt a drive to make sure that others knew the real story of the

Coast Guard. Still, even after he had finished his verses, the captain did not attempt to share his work with others. For reasons known only to him, it would take another four years for him to finish this important chapter of his life.

In 1926, Van Boskerck was the commander of the Bering Sea Forces, headquartered at the remote port of Unalaska, Alaska. Though this was considered a very important command, it had taken the captain to the middle of nowhere. For two years he awoke every day to a cold, unforgiving, barren landscape. Still, while the environment could not have been less inspiring, the dedication and hard work of his crew moved the officer deeply. Here, where the temperature often did not reach above forty below, the Coast Guardsmen performed at levels that awed even Van Boskerck. As he watched them in action, witnessed their selfless dedication, his thoughts were drawn back to the poem he had written four years before. As fate would have it, at about this same time, two visitors from the United States trekked to the snow-covered wilderness outpost. This duo became the key to finishing what Van Boskerck had begun on the *Yamacraw*.

For the captain, Dr. Alf E. Nannestad and Dr. Joseph O. Fourneir were like a breath of spring air. These two men, dentists from the Public Health Department, had come to the great Alaskan Territory to work with the local Eskimo population. One evening, the officer met the men at a local fur trader's home. As if they had known each other their whole lives, the three immediately began to swap stories. The trio soon discovered that they shared a love of literature, poetry, adventure, and music. An old beat-up piano sitting in the corner of the tiny living room seemed to beg them to begin a sing-along. After a few rounds of well-known folk songs, Van

Boskerck recited the words to his "Semper Paratus." The dentists were deeply moved by the old man's thoughts and offered the opinion that if the lyrics were set to music, the captain's message might have a chance to inform all Americans about the importance and the history of the United States Coast Guard.

Well into the long, cold evening, the men beat on the ancient, out-of-tune upright. They also offered a wide variety of opinions as to the melody and the beat needed to fit Van Boskerck's words. It took hours for all of them to agree upon a direction for the music, but when they did make their final call, the song fell together as smoothly as a cruise on a calm sea. For the dentists, "Semper Paratus" was probably little more than an evening well spent, but for the captain, the final product was one of the most important accomplishments of his stellar career.

When he was transferred back to the mainland, Van Boskerck took the finished song to Coast Guard headquarters, playing it for the top brass. They all agreed that this anthem could be of great use to the service branch. It took only a little more effort for the captain to convince his superiors to adopt "Semper Paratus" as the Guard's official anthem. Many of the officers believed that the new song might even become as well known as the navy's "Anchors Aweigh." While never quite achieving the same level of popularity as the navy's anthem, the number, with some rewrites and refinements, has come to define the Coast Guard in a very special fashion. With its upbeat melody and strong lyrics, "Semper Paratus" reflects both the joy and the passion thousands feel about this branch of the service.

If he were alive, Captain Francis Saltus Van Boskerck would no doubt point to today's Coast Guard with great pride. As the roles of the various military branches have changed, and as drug smuggling and terrorism have become the most visible enemies that threaten the liberty that Americans hold so dear, the Coast Guard has reemerged to again become what the founding fathers felt it should be—the final line of defense. In the twenty-first century, this group, more than ever, is "always ready" to ensure that the nation is safe and its shores are secure.

22

THE STARS AND STRIPES FOREVER

etween 1895 and 1918, Sousa's Band, led by the famed "March King," John Philip Sousa, placed twenty-six songs in the era's Top 40. And yes, in the days before radios and music videos, there were playlists that recorded the best-selling music in the United States. One of the few entertainers of any time known by just one name, Sousa was as famous in his day as Elvis, Sinatra, and Madonna were in theirs. Wherever Sousa's Band toured, it played before sold-out crowds who had often waited for hours just to get seats. From coast to coast and even across the Atlantic in Europe, everyone had heard of and could probably hum at least one John Philip Sousa song.

Though it had already sold more than a million wax cylinders, Sousa's Band first topped the charts with "El Capitan March." That song would stay number 1 for seven weeks in the fall of 1895. The group's "King Cotton March" would hit number 2 the same year. A few weeks later Sousa's

"Washington Post (March)" would rule playlists for three weeks. And the song that would become the March King's most popular tune and go on to become the official march of the United States of America would top the chart for the first time in 1897 and then again in 1901. This release would become so wildly popular and so influential that a century later it was still being played by almost every marching band in the country and is as closely identified with the Marine Corps Band as the service unit's own hymn. Yet this incredibly triumphant song, a number that seems to wrap itself in red, white, and blue, was inspired by one of the most tragic events in Sousa's life and literally conceived thousands of miles away from where the Stars and Stripes normally flew.

Sousa, the son of a Marine Corps musician, was born November 6, 1854, in Washington, D.C. The boy must have been a great deal like his father. Music seemed to flow from his soul even before he learned to walk. He could play any musical instrument. After grade school, young Sousa studied violin under noted teacher John Esputa Jr. The boy was so talented on this and a wide range of other instruments that he had an offer to turn professional at thirteen. He might have been playing for the "Greatest Show on Earth" if his father hadn't convinced him to continue his studies by joining the Marine Corps Band. He would remain with the military ensemble until his twentieth birthday. After turning in his uniform, Sousa would spend the next decade playing with several theater orchestras; working as a composer, arranger, and proofreader for a publisher; and writing a musical. He was touring with his own show and appearing in St. Louis, Missouri, when his country called. The successful composer and performer was asked to give up his career and accept the position as the bandmaster for the United States Marines. Many men would have refused the offer, but then many had not been raised in a military family where service to your country was considered the highest and most honored responsibility ever given to a citizen. Dropping everything, Sousa left St. Louis on October 1, 1880.

Because he had spent most of his adult life working in popular music, Sousa understood American tastes better than most military bandleaders. Almost immediately the bandmaster departed from the traditional military numbers of the past, in the process tossing out a great deal of tradition, and brought in new arrangements of popular and classical numbers. The young man then set up a new order for his band. In the past the Marine Corps Band had little resembled regular military duty. It was looked upon as a soft and easy job. Sousa now demanded strict discipline and pushed each of his members to expand his range and talents. He was satisfied with nothing but the best, and he wanted his group to look, act, and sound like the finest military unit of any kind in the country. Under his leadership, within just two years, the Marine Corps Band became the nation's premiere musical ensemble. The President's Band, as it was often called, was now booked into the finest theaters in the country.

In 1886, Sousa began to compose many of the band's marches. More than a few critics believed that the bandmaster had peaked when he wrote "Semper Fidelis," the number that would become the official march of the marines. Yet this familiar tune was really just the beginning of what would become one of the most heralded portfolios of musical works ever attributed to a single American. For the next two decades, Sousa would be on a musical roll.

In 1890, the already wildly popular Sousa helped launch a brand-new industry. The conductor agreed to become one of the first artists at the Columbia Recording Company and to record some of the label's first titles. Under his direction, in just seven years, the Marine Corps Band released more than four hundred different recordings, many of them Sousa's own compositions. It is a little-known fact that some of America's first recording superstars wore marine uniforms.

Now, thanks in part to its success on records, the Marine Corps Band's national tours sold out from coast to coast. Yet though he had created the sensation, Sousa felt a need to stretch his creative wings in new directions.

In 1892, John Philip Sousa retired as director of the marine band and formed his own civilian group. One of the first men who came on board was his good friend and the group's new manager, Robert Blakely. With Sousa hiring the musicians, writing and arranging the music, and conducting the orchestra, and with Blakely running the business end, Sousa's Band quickly became one of the best-known and -loved groups in the world. For the next ten years the bandmaster and his ensemble would play before millions of people and rule the playlists in both America and Europe. Sousa's Band would even surpass the popularity of the Marine Corps Band. To millions it was the musical voice of a nation. Finally, after more than a decade of constant touring with the marines and his own group, Sousa decided to turn his band over to his trusted friend Blakely and take an overdue vacation. He not only wanted to spend time with his family, but he also wanted to see the world as a tourist, not a performer.

Sousa relished his time away from his work. The days he spent as a tourist in Europe were as refreshing as anything he had done in years. Each moment he was away from the grind of entertaining, he could feel his batteries being recharged and his creative spirit coming back to life. How he looked forward to coming back to America and sharing with his friends and his band the stories of his tour. Yet the bliss and relief that Sousa felt were suddenly dashed when he received a telegram. As he carefully read the message, a dark cloud covered his heart. Robert Blakely, the manager of Sousa's Band and in some ways the lifeblood of the group, had unexpectedly died. Now members of the band were wondering if the upcoming national tour would be canceled. Theater managers also were asking how Blakely's death would affect the Sousa's Band schedule. For Sousa the news was not just a shock and a tragedy, but a challenge. Cutting short his vacation, Sousa returned to America in an attempt to reorganize and stabilize the nation's most beloved musical group and find out if he could fill the huge shoes left by his close friend's death.

The bandmaster booked passage on a ship called the *Teutonic*. Unable to rest, Sousa paced the passenger ship's deck for hours each day. With everything in his world so bleak and ominous, Sousa should have been humming funeral dirges. After all, it was his friend who had urged him to leave the marines and go out on his own, where he had found so much of his success. Now there was a void so large that it overwhelmed even the great Sousa. Yet as he strolled, it was Blakely's incredibly optimistic spirit that pushed into his consciousness.

Over the next few days, this tune played out in Sousa's head during his every waking moment. By the time the *Teutonic* landed in New York, the little melody had grown into a fully arranged score, with a huge band blasting each note inside Sousa's brain.

"Throughout the whole tense voyage," Sousa would later write, "that imaginary band continued to unfold the same themes, echoing and re-echoing the most distinct melody. I did not transfer a note of that music to paper while I was on the steamer, but when we reached shore, I set down the measures that my brain-band had been playing for me, and not a note of it has ever changed."

After setting it on paper, arranging it, and teaching it to his band, Sousa used this new march as the triumphant conclusion to each stop of the national tour. Adding words to his music, the bandmaster then created an unforgettable patriotic song that would become an American sensation. Within a decade every band in the country was playing "The Stars and Stripes Forever." By World War I, it was the most popular patriotic march tune in the United States. This song, inspired by the spirit of a departed close friend, remains the most played marching band number even into the twenty-first century.

In 1932, Sousa conducted the United States Marine Corps Band for the final time. In Washington Square, Captain Taylor Branson, the band's director, called Sousa from the crowd and asked him to lead the President's Band in the stirring strains of "The Stars and Stripes Forever." He was now an elderly man, but when Sousa picked up the baton, the years seemed to fall away. It was a young man who directed the music that day. And when the last note had been played, it was a young man who acknowledged the standing ovation he received from both the crowd and the musicians.

A few weeks later, on March 6, 1932, Sousa was conducting a rehearsal of the Ringgold Band at Reading, Pennsylvania. After leading the group in "The Stars and Stripes Forever," he suddenly fell ill. Within hours he was dead. His body was returned to Washington and placed in the Band Hall at Marine Barracks. Four days later, two companies of marines and sailors, the Marine Corps Band,

and honorary pallbearers from the army, navy, and marines led Sousa home. The bandmaster was buried at the Congressional Cemetery. Fifty years later the marines would rename its band hall for Sousa, and on December 10, 1987, "The Stars and Stripes Forever" would finally be named the "Official March of the United States."

23

THE STAR-SPANGLED BANNER

"The Star-Spangled Banner" may very well be both the most beloved and the most despised song in the world. This anthem, born in the midst of an unexpected victory, matched to a British drinking tune, is the musical representation of American democratic ideas. Its words reveal the stubborn pride and undying hope and faith that so identify the nation's people and attitudes. This song and the banner it describes have been an inspiration to its citizens and its allies, as well as a symbol of fear to those who have challenged the nation that sings this anthem and flies the Stars and Stripes.

During the Revolutionary War, the United States had lost many government documents when the British burned public buildings. As the War of 1812 began, most states moved important papers to hidden locations away from government seats. Maryland transported its records from Annapolis to Upper Marlboro and appointed Dr. William Beanes to hide these documents and keep them safe. At least some of these papers were kept in the building housing the city's jail.

For two years, Beanes did a wonderful job minding the documents of the people. Few of his friends even knew the location of the papers, and the British, who had passed through the town on several occasions, had no idea that Upper Marlboro was housing a great number of Maryland's state documents. Yet though he had befriended and treated many wounded English soldiers, by late August 1814, the old doctor had had his fill of redcoats. When he discovered two British infantrymen drunk and staggering along Upper Marlboro's downtown streets, he reacted in a rage. Beanes arrested the soldiers and tossed them into jail. Then, compounding his problems, the doctor allowed one of the men to escape. That English trooper brought the British army back to the town. It is a wonder that the angry commanding officer did not demand that Upper Marlboro be burned to the ground because of Beanes's defiance of the Crown. Instead, the army freed the lone remaining prisoner while somehow failing to note the significance of the boxes of documents a stone's throw from the cell, and then took the doctor back to Baltimore to be tried as a political prisoner.

Fearing for the life of their beloved physician, a group of city leaders from Upper Marlboro rode to Georgetown to enlist the help of a lawyer. The man they sought out to provide this legal counsel was Francis Scott Key. Key was not only one of the area's top attorneys, but as an army veteran, he was familiar with the special circumstances involved in the arrest of Dr. Beanes. He also knew British law.

At that moment America was on the brink of losing the war. The capital city, Washington, had just been burned by the British. President James Madison and his wife, Dolly, had barely escaped being captured. Now the important American port of Baltimore was

Oh, say, can you see, by the dawn's
early light,
What so proudly we hail'd at the
twilight's last gleaming?
Whose broad stripes and
bright stars, thro' the perilous
fight,
O'er the ramparts we watch'd, were
so gallantly streaming?
And the rockets' red glare, the
bombs bursting in air,
Gave proof thro' the night that our
flag was still there.
O say, does that star-spangled banner yet wave
O'er the land of the free and the
home of the brave?

On the shore dimly seen thro' the
mists of the deep,
Where the foe's haughty host in
dread silence reposes,
What is that which the breeze, o'er
the towering steep,
As it fitfully blows, half conceals,
half discloses?
Now it catches the gleam of the
morning's first beam,
In full glory reflected, now shines
on the stream:

'Tis the star-spangled banner: O,
long may it wave
O'er the land of the free and the
home of the brave!

And where is that band who so
vauntingly swore
That the havoc of war and the battle's confusion
A home and a country should leave
us no more?
Their blood has wash'd out their
foul footsteps' pollution.
No refuge could save the hireling
and slave
From the terror of flight or the
gloom of the grave:
And the star-spangled banner in triumph doth wave
O'er the land of the free and the
home of the brave.

O, thus be it ever when freemen
shall stand,
Between their lov'd homes and the
war's desolation;
Blest with vict'ry and peace, may
the heav'n-rescued land
Praise the Pow'r that hath made
and preserv'd us as a nation!

fut

Then conquer we must, when our cause is just,
And this be our motto: "In God is our trust"

And the star-spangled banner in triumph shall wave
O'er the land of the free and the home of the brave!

readying itself for a massive British assault. With the English navy and army preparing to lay ruin to the city, it hardly seemed the right time for Key to seek the release of the elderly doctor. Yet, even though the odds seemed long, the lawyer contacted Colonel John Skinner, an American agent for prisoner exchange, and on September 3 the two of them set sail for Baltimore on a tiny sloop. Four days later they received permission to board the British ship *Tonnant* and were given an audience with Admiral Alexander Cochrane. The men then discussed the case against Dr. Beanes.

The British officer dismissed Key almost as soon as he presented his request for a dismissal of charges. Both the attorney and Skinner were then ordered back onto their boat. Key had anticipated that his request would initially be turned down, so he had prepared a backup plan. Before he could be escorted from the *Tonnant,* the lawyer produced a packet of letters written by British soldiers who had been treated by Dr. Beanes. These testimonials swayed the admiral's judgment and won the case for the Americans. Cochrane ordered that Beanes be freed, but because the Americans now knew some of the British plans for attack, the men could not leave the harbor until the battle was concluded. Until such time, the doctor, Key, and Skinner would remain guests of the Royal Navy. Even as they were placed back on their own sloop, the Americans were ordered to stay anchored beside the English warships. Hence, the men would not be formally released until September 16.

The bombardment of Baltimore and Fort McHenry began just after dawn on September 13, 1814. For twenty-five hours the British fleet unleashed a relentless attack, lobbing 1,500 bombshells weighing over two hundred pounds each at the American fort. It was a spectacular show, but it was not very effective. As Key, Beanes, and Skinner observed, many of those bombs blew up in the air long before they struck their intended targets. The bombs were not the only English weapons that failed that day. From very small boats the Brits fired Congreve rockets that traced wobbly arcs of red flame across the sky. Yet, because the harbor was filled with almost two dozen ships the Americans had already sunk, the English navy could not get close enough to place the rockets in realistic range of their targets. So most of the flaming darts fell harmlessly into the water.

As they waited eight miles from the fort, Key, Skinner, and Beanes had no idea what was really happening. Because the skies were filled with fire and smoke, and the destructive force of the Royal Naval seemed awesome, the men were convinced that the American forces were taking a mighty pounding. Still, they assumed because the shelling continued throughout the night that Fort McHenry had not surrendered. Just before dawn on the fourteenth, the British quit firing and all was quiet. The American detainees looked toward the distant fort and saw flames coming from the American outpost. They believed that Baltimore and Fort McHenry had fallen to the enemy.

As the sun began to light the new day, a depressed Key held a telescope to his eye and peered through the smoke and haze. What he expected to see were the ruins of Fort McHenry. What he spied took his breath away. Though he was eight miles from the fort, he clearly saw an American flag flying atop a huge flagpole. He had never witnessed anything so triumphantly beautiful. Many who had never seen the port believed it a miracle that by using a crude spyglass Key could see the fort's colors. To this day, many don't understand how, from a distance of eight miles, Key could have seen the Stars and Stripes.

A year before the battle, the defiant American officer had asked Mary Young Pickersgill, a Baltimore flag maker, to sew a banner so large that the British would be able to see it flying for miles. Pickersgill and her daughter used four hundred yards of bunting, cut stars that were twenty-six inches across, and created a flag that had eight red and seven white stripes, each two feet wide. By the time the Pickersgills finished their work, the Stars and Stripes was forty-two feet wide and thirty feet high. When the flag flew at the top of the fort's ninety-foot pole, it was a sight that no one could miss. On that September morning, it boldly signaled that the Americans had withstood the best the British had to offer and that their banner had not even dipped, much less fallen.

Key had dabbled in poetry since his youth. As he stood on the old sloop, the sight of the American flag billowing in the wind inspired him. He pulled a letter from his pocket and began to jot down his emotions and set them to verse on the paper's blank side. He continued his writing two days later when he sailed into Baltimore. The lawyer finally finished and polished his poem while staying at the city's Indian Queen Hotel.

One of those impressed by what Key had written was his

brother-in-law, Judge J. H. Nicholson. It was Nicholson who took the verses to a local printer and had Key's words printed on a hand-bill. The poem was circulated throughout the city under the title "Defence of Fort M'Henry." On September 20, the *Baltimore Patriot* published the poem, and over the next few weeks Key's work popped up in scores of newspapers up and down the Atlantic Coast. It quickly became a great source of inspiration for the American cause. Yet it was still just a poem, not a song.

Two years before he had penned his ode about the American victory at Fort McHenry, Key had written another poem saluting the life of Commodore Stephen Decatur. He had set those verses to an English melody called "An Anacreon in Heaven." The original song, probably composed by John Stafford Smith around 1780, was used by the English Anacreontic Club as their unofficial pub tune. As each of his new poem's verses matched the pub song's meter and length, Key might have had the "Anacreon" melody in mind when he wrote his words describing the Battle of Fort McHenry. Whether the music came to him on the sloop that morning or later when he reworked his poem remains unknown, but within a month the lawyer's words had been linked to that music. In October, Baltimore actor Ferdinand Durang first sang the new song at Captain McCauley's tavern. A few months later, in early 1815, the anthem was again published, this time complete with music; it had also been renamed "The Star-Spangled Banner."

For more than a century "The Star-Spangled Banner" was used by the United States Army and Navy as the national anthem. Yet until the Hoover administration, the United States did not recognize Key's work as being anything more than just another patriotic song. Finally, in 1931, by an act of Congress, the song that described one of the nation's most inspiring moments was made the official anthem of the United States.

The use of "The Star-Spangled Banner" before sporting events and other public celebrations is a fairly recent development too. It was during Word War II that the playing of Key's song began to become a part of American tradition at public gatherings. Even then, many felt that the overuse of the anthem would lead to trivializing its meaning. Some wanted the playing of the "Banner" to be saved for only special government events. Yet by the end of World War II, the tradition had been established and there was no turning back.

There are two copies of the original Baltimore broadsheet that first brought Key's poem to the world. One is in the hands of the Maryland Historical Society; the other resides at the Library of Congress. The flag that inspired the song, now tattered and faded, hangs in the Smithsonian Institution's Museum of American History. Over the years, before it was made a part of the American trust, many citizens cut pieces of the old banner for souvenirs. Because of this, the flag that so proudly presented the fifteen stars and fifteen stripes at Fort McHenry is now just thirty by thirty-four feet. But, thanks to a careful restoration process, it is still on display for all Americans to see.

On January 11, 1843, long before his song became the musical symbol for the nation he so loved, Francis Scott Key died in Baltimore. Today his remains rest at the Mount Olivet Cemetery in Frederick, Maryland. A spotlighted American flag flies over his grave twenty-four hours a day, and the song he created still represents the power, majesty, and pride of the United States that the lawyer noted at Fort McHenry in 1814.

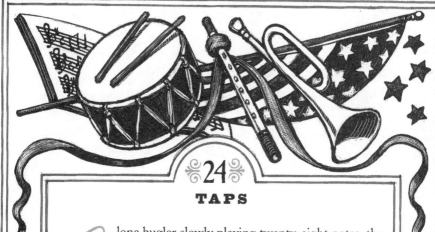

TAPS

a lone bugler slowly playing twenty-eight notes, the mournful sounds of his instrument carrying across a darkening night and immersing those who hear these strains in deep, somber thought. Such is the very nature of the bugle solo we know as "Taps."

The simple melody that is "Taps" seems to define a sense of loss better than any words ever have. No master of literature has ever come close to conveying the emotions of the death of a friend or family member as well as this tune. "Taps" is recognized as one of the saddest songs ever performed. There is no doubt that millions have first realized the heartfelt impact of loss when they heard this tune played.

To most Americans, "Taps" represents a final salute to a past life, a last good-bye to someone who served his or her country with distinction. The generation that survived World War II recalls the bugler blowing "Taps" at President Franklin Delano Roosevelt's funeral. They heard that African American musician over the radio or caught him in newsreels. *Life* magazine ran the bugler's photo so that all could see the tears streaming down his face as he played.

Baby boomers will probably always remember seeing and hearing the song on television as it was used as a final tribute to President John Fitzgerald Kennedy. Recently "Taps" was also played to memorialize young men who died in the war against terrorism in Afghanistan, as well as at the funerals of many of the policemen and firemen who lost their lives on 9/11. Yet even though tradition supports the image of "Taps" being a funeral song, its origins are really much different.

Unlike many military music pieces used in America, such as reveille, "Taps" was not imported and adapted from Europe; rather, this tune was composed and originated in the United States. It came about because of a specific need. Prior to the invention of the shortwave radio and walkie-talkies, the infantry and cavalry communicated through a variety of means ranging from carrier pigeon to signal flags to bugle calls. For thousands of years the latter marked the moment to make an advance or a charge and the time to pull back or retreat. By the Civil War, bugle calls were also used to wake troops up in the morning, to signal that it was time for a meal at noon, and to let them know when they needed to go to bed at night. The lights-out call or final call of the day was always called "Taps," even though a number of different tunes were used for this call by various divisions and branches of the military.

In 1861, most Union buglers played a melody from Silas Casey's book *Tactics* to signal that it was time for bed. Not everyone liked this song, and because there were no set regulations requiring the piece from *Tactics* as the final call, some commanding officers ordered their buglers to play other tunes in its place. In midsummer

Fading light dims the sight,
And a star gems the sky, gleaming
bright.
From afar drawing nigh—Falls the
night.

Day is done, gone the sun,
From the lake, from the hills, from
the sky.

All is well, safely rest, God is
nigh.

Then good night, peaceful night,
Till the light of the dawn shineth
bright,
God is near, do not fear—Friend,
good night.

1862, General Daniel Butterfield issued an order that would ultimately change the final call at every United States military post and
camp around the world.

General Butterfield, the leader of Meroll's Division, Fitz-John
Porter's Corps, Army of the Potomac, had been told that the melody
from Casey's book being used for his last call was actually a French
tune. The general didn't believe that American men should be called
anywhere at anytime by anything other than a melody written by not
just an American, but an American who was loyal to the Union
cause. With this in mind, Butterfield undertook the task of composing a new call himself. When he finished, he sent for his own bugler.
The bugler would later write a letter to a historical society that
included his memories of that day and the manner in which the Butterfield song actually spread across the Civil War fronts.

> *One day, soon after the seven days battles on the Peninsular,*
> *when the Army of the Potomac was lying in camp at Harrison's*
> *Landing, General Daniel Butterfield, then commanding our*
> *Brigade, sent for me, and showing me some notes on a staff writ-*
> *ten in pencil on the back of an envelope, asked me to sound them*
> *on my bugle. I did this several times, playing the music as writ-*
> *ten. He changed it somewhat, lengthening some notes and short-*
> *ening others, but retaining the melody as he first gave it to me.*
> *After getting it to his satisfaction, he directed me to sound that*
> *call for Taps thereafter in place of the regulation call.*
>
> *The music was beautiful on that still summer night, and*
> *was heard far beyond the limits of our Brigade. The next day I*
> *was visited by several buglers from neighboring Brigades, asking*
> *for copies of the music which I gladly furnished.*

I think no general order was issued from army headquarters authorizing the substitution of this for the regulation call, but as each brigade commander exercised his own discretion in such minor matters, the call was gradually taken up through the Army of the Potomac.

Butterfield was probably more of an arranger than a composer. Military research eventually traced the basic melody to another call known as "Scott's Tattoo," which had been used to inform men that it was one hour before all lights were to be extinguished. Still, it was Butterfield who lifted the tune from obscurity and positioned it to become one of the two best-known bugle calls in America.

For several months "Taps" was used only as a lights-out call. As many men didn't know how to tell time and even fewer had pocket watches, this new bugle call became a trusty clock for hundreds of thousands of Union troops. As the battle lines of the North and South were also very close together and as fighting usually ended at dusk, there can be little doubt that many wearing gray also grew to depend upon the Union bugle call to signal that it was time for bed. It was this proximity of lines during the War between the States that led to using "Taps" for something much more grave than a good-night call.

In late 1862, a Union cannoneer was killed in action. As was often the case, a grave was dug near the place where he fell. Military protocol required that the soldier be honored with a traditional three-volley salute from members of a rifle brigade. In this case, following those regulations would have put the rest of the troops at great risk. The men in blue were outnumbered and hiding in woods while waiting for reinforcements. Captain John C. Tidball of Battery

A, Second Artillery, knew that the rifle salute would probably mean death to the rest of the group. So he signaled for the guns to remain silent and ordered that "Taps" be used to honor and bid farewell to the beloved comrade. Thus began the use of "Taps" as a way of signaling not just the end of day, but the end of a life.

This real story of "Taps" has long been overshadowed by a legend that has grown up around the song. This folklore, which dates back to the time when Butterfield arranged and ordered the playing of the bugle call for the first time, is so elaborate, heart wrenching, and seemingly well documented with dates and names that it is often accepted as the truth.

The story revolved around a Union officer named Robert Ellicombe. In 1862, at Harrison's Landing, Virginia, the captain supposedly heard the cries of an injured soldier lying somewhere just out of sight. As the battle lines were ragged at best and men from the North and South were all but mingling in the fog, the captain could not have known if the calls came from a friend or an enemy. Even though it was an unwise thing to do, it was said that he crawled to the spot where the man lay. He then dragged the wounded solider back to his camp. Before a doctor could be summoned, the trooper died. When Ellicombe finally looked at the Confederate soldier's face, he realized that the young man was actually his own son.

Legend has it that the bereaved captain asked his superiors for permission to bury his son with full military honors, but the request was denied. So rather than volleys of gunfire fired over the young man's grave, Ellicombe played a piece of music he had found in his son's pocket. The father believed his son, a musician, had composed the twenty-eight-note melody. Supposedly the name jotted on top of the notes was "Taps."

Could this story be based on fact? Possibly, and in this case there is a fairly easy way to connect the truth to this legend.

While it can be ascertained that Ellicombe's son did not compose the piece, perhaps he had jotted down the music after hearing it played across enemy lines. It is also possible that he had transcribed those notes to share with Confederate buglers. If so, then this proves that even during a period when millions of Americans were fighting each other to the death, the universality of this bugle call was felt and embraced by men who represented both sides. As in the case of the captain and his son, it remains a very sad historic irony that when each Civil War battle was finished, "Taps" would unite men from the North and South in death, even if nothing could bring them together in life.

There are many sets of lyrics that have been added to this bugle call over the years. While the most popular are printed here, "Taps" will never really be known as anything more than an instrumental, for no words can express the sadness of the last call of life as well as the haunting strains of a bugler playing twenty-eight very simple notes.

25

THIS IS MY COUNTRY

his Is My Country" has probably been sung by more high school choirs than any other patriotic song. It is a standard at Independence Day celebrations, Memorial Day concerts, and Veterans Day services. Yet this song that is so well known and so deeply loved by millions has never been on a hit-parade chart or been honored with a gold record. Of the modern American patriotic classics, it stands alone as a choral and band piece, so rarely recorded by an individual artist that it is usually impossible to find a copy of the song at even the largest music outlets.

In 1940, most Americans knew that the United States would eventually be dragged into the Second World War. As we were already doing everything in our power via financial aid and manufacturing to help the British and French, there was no secret as to whose side we were on. Our military was beginning to gear up for war as officers drilled troops on an almost daily basis. Even President Roosevelt and Congress were turning their attention away from the programs that halted the depression to bills that built our readiness to fight Hitler and his armies.

In Hollywood, the military buildup and rumors of war were influencing the motion pictures being produced by the major studios. Jimmy Cagney's *The Fighting 69th* gave the nation a glimpse of war by looking back at the First World War. Meanwhile, other new pictures took dramatic looks at the war in Europe and the Far East. Among these were Tyrone Power starring in *A Yank in the RAF,* Dennis Morgan leading the way in *Captain of the Clouds,* and a John Wayne epic about Americans flying planes for China in the Asian war against Japan, *The Fighting Tigers.* So, long before Pearl Harbor, thanks in large measure to Hollywood, Americans were getting used to the images of war.

One of those who was given the task of writing many of the songs that were a part of these productions was Don Raye. When the Andrews Sisters landed major roles in Abbott and Costello's *Buck Privates,* Raye joined with Hughie Prince to compose one of the best-remembered and most beloved novelty songs of the 1940s. "Boogie Woogie Bugle Boy" would become a favorite on jukeboxes and radio stations and at USO shows throughout the entire war. Though the Andrews Sisters would score dozens of other hits, it was this military number, and their constant and untiring work for the USO during World War II, that made them America's most popular sister act and heroes and sweethearts to GIs everywhere.

When not joining with Prince, Raye worked with a number of other songwriters producing a long list of hits including "Beat Me Daddy, Eight to the Bar," "Hey, Mr. Postman," "Cow-Cow Boogie," and "House of Blue Lights." But it was a number he penned with Al

Jacobs in 1940 that would become the most performed song in his large portfolio.

Unlike Raye, who usually composed songs with unique beats and unusual lyrics, Jacobs made his name with traditional love songs. "Hurt," "Every Day of My Life," and "I Need You Now" were a few of his hits. Though the songwriting team had seen scores of different artists from a wide range of different music styles record their compositions, it is doubtful that either Jacobs or Raye would have dreamed that a song they came together to write would be introduced to the world by a man whose name was well known to all facets of the music-buying American audience.

Long before Fred Waring earned the title of the "Man Who Taught America How to Sing," he was an inventor. Even as a child, he constantly conceived ideas about machines that could improve individuals' lives. Yet though he was an engineering whiz, it was music that always controlled his life.

As a teen, when the U.S. troops were still fighting the First World War, Waring formed the Waring-McClintock Snap Orchestra. A few years later, as a part of Waring's Banjo Orchestra, the young man toured a large portion of the country. When he was majoring in architecture at Penn State University, music was still such a part of his life that he quit school just short of a degree and hit the road with Waring's Pennsylvanians. By the late twenties the band was so hot that Hollywood called, and Waring made appearances in some of the country's first talking pictures.

After Waring's Pennsylvanians, now a fifty-five-piece jazz orchestra, completed a record-breaking six-month run at New York's Roxy Theatre, the band was given its own network radio program.

For the next two decades, the Pennsylvanians were a mainstay on the airwaves. Their leader, Waring, was a musical pioneer, the first major orchestra leader to use a girl singer, to feature vocalists with an orchestra, and to combine orchestra and glee clubs. Meanwhile, Waring the songwriter wrote more than ninety college fight songs and scores of patriotic numbers. He and his orchestra would also record more than fifteen hundred songs during that period. Between 1923 and 1954, the band would land fifty-three singles in the nation's Top 40. The group scored this astounding number of hits in spite of the fact that the Pennsylvanians quit recording for a decade between 1933 and 1943. Yet though he was one of the most honored musicians of his era, Waring is best remembered for something he did in his spare time.

At his home workshop, the musician invented the Waring blender. An instant hit, the device revolutionized life in kitchens, bars, and malt shops. When Waring added the instant steam iron to his list of inventions, his fame was assured. It goes without saying that his ideas are still being used today. Though he could have made a fortune in industry, Waring always returned to his real love, music. And it was there, with a song from Raye and Jacobs, that the bandleader probably touched America even more deeply than he did with his inventions.

In 1940, Don Raye and Al Jacobs put together a formula number that was probably inspired by Kate Smith's monster hit "God Bless America." At that time a host of different artists were looking for a song that could create the kind of national sensation that Smith had when she had released the Irving Berlin song. Raye and Jacobs's "This Is My Country" would have seemed the perfect vehicle to make a run up radio playlists, except for one problem: "This Is My

Country" did not work very well as a solo piece. It was not a song that Bing Crosby, Rudy Vallee, or Fats Waller could sell. It was also not a song that worked with the great dance bands of the era like Guy Lombardo's, Tommy Dorsey's, Glen Miller's, or Benny Goodman's. Even small ensembles, such as the Andrews Sisters, could not really do justice to the simple majesty of the piece. Ironically, one of the few men who had both an orchestra and a large vocal group was not recording at the time. Nevertheless, "This Is My Country" ended up in Fred Waring's hands.

Waring, whose radio shows were as much about education as they were entertainment, loved the new Raye and Jacobs song. Essentially, Waring believed his musical calling in life was to revive the nation's interest in the kind of group singing that had been so popular in the preradio days. As Mitch Miller would do on television, Waring devoted much of his programs to, as he would say, "songs normal folks could sing along" with the band.

In a 1940 broadcast, Waring's Pennsylvanians did a superb job of bringing "This Is My Country" to life. Letters poured in to the network asking the band to play it again and again. When war did break out, "This Is My Country" became an almost weekly offering to a nation in need of inspiration. If the Pennsylvanians had been releasing singles at the time, there is little doubt that the song would have been a huge hit.

While there were no record sales generated by Waring's performance, sheet-music sales went through the roof. High school and college choirs across the nation wanted to perform "This Is My Country." Thanks to Waring's arrangement and radio performances of "This Is My Country," at many concerts audiences stood and sang along with whomever was performing the song. By 1943, in New

York colleges, in rural Illinois schools, in Alabama churches, in California movie studios, and even on battlefields in Europe and the Pacific, "This Is My Country" became almost as well known and much sung as "The Star-Spangled Banner." It was one of the few patriotic numbers whose popularity remained strong after the war ended.

Today the Raye-Jacobs piece is still a choral favorite. It has probably remained so popular thanks to its unique combination of majesty and simplicity. While its music and its words soar, its message and its melody are within reach of almost everyone who can carry a tune. There is also one more bit of inspired genius that makes "This Is My Country" so special.

In most nations, patriotic songs are not written in the first person. Most people don't sing of "my" country, it is "our" country. Don Raye and Al Jacobs knew that Americans staked a unique and individual claim as the owners of the land where they lived. Thus, "This Is My Country" was a song not just for all Americans, but for each American. In that way, it was much more personal than even "God Bless America."

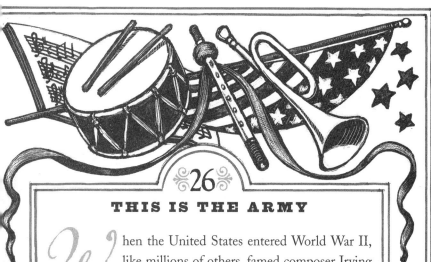

26

THIS IS THE ARMY

W hen the United States entered World War II, like millions of others, famed composer Irving Berlin felt a need to serve his country. Yet at fifty-three, the legend of Broadway was too old to join any branch of the armed services, so Berlin sought out another approach that would put his talents to work in a way that could raise morale while earning money for the war effort. The composer figured that if he could not go overseas to participate in the war effort, then he would bring the war to the home front via a musical production.

During World War I, Berlin had produced *Yip! Yip! Yaphank!* That Broadway production had been a vehicle for fund-raising and had produced a wide array of tunes that helped lift spirits both on the home front and on battlefields in Europe. The showman figured if it had worked a generation before, then a musical would work now as well.

As one of the most powerful men in the world of entertainment, Berlin was very well connected. Though the few civilians who had to meet with General George Marshall usually waited weeks on their appointment, like industrial giants such as Henry Ford, Berlin had no problem simply picking up the phone and calling one of the military's most powerful leaders. It also took only a few minutes for Marshall to approve Berlin's request to use enlisted army personnel in the production. So at a time when almost every available man was being shipped overseas, the composer got to pick more than three hundred GIs to serve in his new New York–based production.

After visiting with Marshall, Berlin put together his production team and moved his offices to Camp Upton, New York. This was the same location where he had done preproduction work for *Yip! Yip! Yaphank!* In the spring of 1942, just months after Pearl Harbor, the composer began to knock out tunes on an old piano in a dusty Civilian Conservation Corps barracks. One of the songs he wrote there probably did a better job of explaining the dramatic change from civilian life to military life than anything anyone had ever before written. "God Bless America" might have been much more inspiring, but, in truth, this number was far more creative and much better written.

"This Is the Army" was a masterpiece. The lyrics painted a humorous but fairly complete picture of the transition each new recruit had to make when he left home and entered the military. While the story and words might have carried a comedic edge, they also rang true. Every one of the men who rolled into Berlin's camp to work in the production could easily identify with the song's message. As the composer would soon discover, millions of others would consider this number the definitive "letter home" explaining what the jump into the army or navy or marines really meant.

While the theme struck an honest note, the music to "This Is the Army" might have been the key to the song's incredible reception. In his great wisdom, Berlin wrote a melody that almost anyone could remember and, most important, with its rather modest range, almost anyone could sing. Thus, while it would be the anchor of his entire show, "This Is the Army" had the potential to move off Broadway and into every boot camp and battlefront in the world.

This Is the Army premiered on Broadway on July 4, 1942. It was scheduled to run four weeks, but the show was so good that it sold out through the end of September. Eleanor Roosevelt had seen the show three times during its run and was so enthralled with it that she requested that Berlin bring *This Is the Army* to Washington so her husband could see it too. FDR personally thanked each man in the troupe for making the show such a success. As it turned out, Washington and the presidential performance were just the beginning.

This Is the Army would continue to tour, first in the United States for a year, then overseas in war zones, until the end of the war. Ultimately, simply by using his immense talents, enthusiasm, and connections, Berlin would raise millions of dollars for the Army Emergency Relief Fund.

In 1943, the show was even turned into a movie hit by Warner Brothers, starring future president Ronald Reagan and the "Sweetheart of the Hollywood Canteen," Joan Leslie. The movie was even a bigger hit than the Broadway play, earning more than $10 million, all given directly to the relief fund.

The song "This Is the Army" would become a Top 40 single in both 1942 and 1943. Popular recording artists Hal McIntryre and Horace Heidt would each take the song into the nation's Top 20. Yet even though it sold hundreds of thousands of records and was a radio and jukebox favorite, the song was never intended to be identified with a solo artist. "This Is the Army" was meant to be every serviceman's anthem, and that is the way it would remain.

On October 22, 1945, on the island of Maui, a full two months after the war ended, Irving Berlin concluded his final appearance in the live production of *This Is the Army* by saying he hoped he would never again have to write another war song. As it turned out, he didn't. Yet along with "God Bless America" and "White Christmas," "This Is the Army" struck a universal chord with both military personnel and civilians. In a stroke of genius, the man who composed more than a thousand songs managed to create a lighthearted standard that embraced the love of country, a sense of duty, and the need to sacrifice better than most of the other songs that came out during World War II.

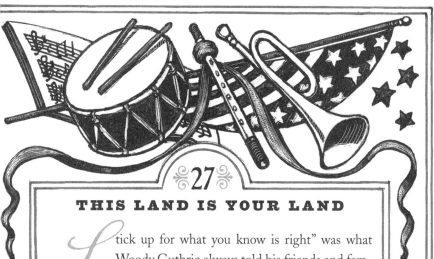

27

THIS LAND IS YOUR LAND

*S*tick up for what you know is right" was what Woody Guthrie always told his friends and family, as well as those who came to listen to him sing. The renowned folksinger lived those words as well. For more than two decades, he stood up for unpopular causes throughout the United States. The singer took these controversial stands because he felt the pain of those who had been forgotten, neglected, pushed aside, and cast out. He was a voice of America's poorest people at a time when being anti-establishment wasn't popular. Guthrie's concern and protest were revealed again and again in his music.

During his life and even today, there are many who debate who Woody Guthrie was and what he stood for, yet there can be little debate that the singer was the father of modern American folk music. His performances and writing inspired the likes of Pete Seeger, Peter, Paul and Mary, and Bob Dylan, as well as thousands of other country and rock musicians. He was to folk music what Hank Williams was to country music and Albert Brumley was to gospel music. This, in spite of the fact that he remained largely unknown during his own life.

For years Guthrie was ignored by the musical establishment because of his communist leanings and his seeming lack of regard for fame, power, money, or status. Though now considered a legend—he has even been inducted into the Songwriters Hall of Fame and the Rock and Roll Hall of Fame—during his life Guthrie was a person feared, a voice whose messages shook the very core of the American establishment. It now seems hard to believe that the man who challenged a nation with his words could have taken his first steps in a tiny backwoods town in the country's heartland.

Woodrow Wilson Guthrie was born on July 14, 1912, in Okemah, Oklahoma. Though well educated, the Guthries were nevertheless poor. Always small for his age, Woody learned how to play guitar and entertain to be accepted by other children. Yet even as a child his efforts to become a part of the mainstream were often futile. Bright, creative, and funny, he seemed destined to become just another average American boy until he was hit with back-to-back tragedies. First his sister died in a fire, and then his mother was institutionalized with Huntington's disease. These events severely changed the boy and his outlook on life. He took on a serious edge and became a loner. Even though he would continue to entertain, he no longer sang to be accepted; he sang to voice his own emotions and ideas.

It was a still-disillusioned Guthrie who left home at sixteen. Married soon after, he found himself ill-prepared to take care of the three children who quickly joined his family. When the depression hit, Guthrie's meager existence dried up altogether. He would soon live out the tales John Steinbeck wrote about in *The Grapes of Wrath*. Woody and his family left the dust bowl and traveled to California looking for the promise of work. They found little promise and a great deal of hostility. As the young man suffered through hunger and persecution, he began to pen songs that reflected the plight of his own experiences as well as the experiences of those he met in his travels. What he saw led to his giving up on the American capitalist model and adopting the mantle of communism. His songs thus took on the causes of migrant workers, women's rights, and unionization. These were far from popular subjects in the entertainment community and mainstream America, but they struck a chord with those like the Okies who had wandered west in search of the promise of a new life. A radio station across the Mexican border allowed Guthrie to beam his musical messages to the United States, and this exposure opened up an audience for the writer's passionate views on society and government. With songs such as "I Ain't Got No Home" and "Pretty Boy Floyd," he touched many nerves as well as landing scores of fans and converts. Yet it meant little to his bank balance or his status. In his own view he was still a struggling outsider, a starving artist in search of the answers to his own search for the meaning of life.

In the late 1930s, Guthrie left the West Coast and moved to New York. There he joined with other revolutionary artists such as Leadbelly and Pete Seeger; he also got to know socially conscious authors like Steinbeck. A few months in this environment made his lyrics sharper and even more pointed. They could now be sung as editorials about the failure of the American system to open its arms to all of its people and to recognize the need to care for the poor and the minorities. Like those elements of society Guthrie was trying to help, his songs were often treated with disdain and contempt.

Though he would constantly pick up his bags and hit the road to roam across the United States, the singer would usually come back and stay in New York. The city with its many people and cultures didn't just call out to him, it inspired him. In the slums and on the streets Guthrie saw how society had failed time and time again. He saw poverty, hunger, crime, class warfare, and abuse firsthand. This meeting of the best and worst of the country would allow the songwriter to combine protest and patriotism in a fashion that was unlike any song ever penned in the United States. Yet it was something else altogether that inspired Guthrie to pick up his pen and write his most revered song.

Wherever Woody traveled in 1940, he could not escape hearing Kate Smith belt out Irving Berlin's "God Bless America" on jukeboxes and radio stations. Guthrie thought the song was the ultimate propaganda tool for the American government he so distrusted. On February 23, in New York City, while staying at the fleabag Hanover House on the corner of Sixth Avenue and Forty-third Street, the songwriter decided to compose what he believed to be a truer version of "God Bless America." On an old piece of notebook paper he took out his frustrations and anger in a musical tour of the country. He wrote his words in symbolic protest of the places where the poor and middle class were not admitted. He concluded each of his six verses with the line "God Blessed America for me," something he hardly believed. He set his lyrics to the old A. P. Carter tune "Little Darlin' Pal of Mine." Then Guthrie put the song away and forgot about it for almost five years.

World War II changed Guthrie. He served for a time in the merchant marine and later the army. He even found some things to love in his own country and government. He still held on to some very left-wing ideas, but the now older and wiser songwriter had become more comfortable with America as it was. The depression was over, times were better, and the war had brought about a unity Guthrie had never before observed. On April 20, 1944, between duties with the merchant marine and the army, he finally cut "This Land Is Your Land." Responding to his more moderate views of the nation, he reworked his Irving Berlin parody by rewriting the last line in each verse. The tag now read "This land was made for you and me."

The song was not immediately released and it probably should have been forgotten. Yet in the years after the war, Guthrie's little protest number was somehow adopted by thousands of those who heard his concerts. The song was then literally passed from person to person, moving across the country like a slow wind. By the time it made its way from New York to Los Angeles, "This Land Is Your Land" had become a patriotic standard, sung in school classes, by church choirs, and on local radio stations by artists of all ages and backgrounds. Within a decade it was proposed that Guthrie's little song replace "The Star-Spangled Banner" as America's official anthem. That never happened, but "This Land Is Your Land" was adopted by those from the right and the left, the poor and the rich, the famous and the infamous as one of this nation's most beloved songs. For reasons that even the writer could not fully understand, "This Land" became the common man's musical "Pledge of Allegiance." Guthrie also discovered that while he had written the song to present the pain he saw in his native land, now most sang it because they saw the promise of America in each word, phrase, and verse.

Guthrie died in 1967, of the same disease that had taken his mother from him when he was boy. Like his mother, he spent most of his last fifteen years in hospitals. For the last decade of his life, he was but a shell of the man who had penned more than a thousand songs and started the modern American folk movement. Yet Guthrie lived long enough to realize that "This Land Is Your Land" had become his biggest and most beloved composition. Guthrie saw "This Land" recorded by hundreds of artists, including Bing Crosby, Tex Ritter, Jay and the Americans, the New Christy Minstrels, the Kingston Trio, and the Mormon Tabernacle Choir. The writer watched in amazement as several different companies used the classic tune for television and radio commercials.

Eight years after his death, in 1975, "This Land Is Your Land" was sung by tens of millions of schoolchildren simultaneously during the first annual "Music in Our Schools Day." This would mark the beginning of the nation's celebration of its bicentennial and would cement the Woody Guthrie tune as an important part of America's 1976 festivities. Somehow, in just a little more than three decades, "This Land" had become as American as baseball, hot dogs, and Yankee Doodle.

For many there is a great irony that a man whose politics were so alien to the majority in the United States could create a song that would so well reflect what this nation's ideals really mean. Yet the fact that Woody Guthrie was not a member of the American mainstream would seem to validate the most basic principles defined by the the founders of this nation. The Revolutionary War was fought to ensure that every man and woman would have the right to voice his or her ideas, opinions, and beliefs without fear of government censorship or retribution. In 1776, this fundamental right was viewed as being central to the American process. "This Land Is Your

Land" proves that the principle and the rights that were fought for at Bunker Hill and Yorktown are still alive. Thanks to those rights, even a voice like Woody Guthrie's can move a nation to realize just how much of a blessing it is to live in a country where the land is really the people's land. He might have written his most famous song for reasons most Americans could not understand—reasons some even considered wrong, but Guthrie got it right: America really does belong to "you and me."

28
THE WASHINGTON POST
(MARCH)

I n the world of band music, a universe where marches played by more than a hundred instrumentalists are the mainstay, one man stands head and shoulders above all others. John Philip Sousa is the king. For more than a hundred years he has held that title, and as long as bands perform at parades, sporting events, and national celebrations, he will probably be recognized as the best in this field. Like Frank Sinatra and Elvis Presley, during his time he defined music, and even though he was born in an era without radio or television, his influence might even outlast that of those two popular music icons of the twentieth century.

Sousa was born on November 6, 1854, in Washington, D.C. The fittingness of the man who probably composed more patriotic music than any other composer being born in the nation's capital makes his story that much more fantastic. The son of immigrant parents, young Sousa was literally surrounded by music from the day of his birth. His father, John

Antonio, played in the Marine Corps Band. This meant that as a child John Philip attended many concerts where the president of the United States sat in the audience listening to the boy's dad play. Seeing his father perform for the most powerful man in the country must have been an exciting experience during times of peace, but during the Civil War, with enemy armies just miles away, these special occasions probably packed even more punch. On occasions, Sousa watched Abraham Lincoln deeply moved by the concerts. The boy had to come away from those experiences realizing the power of music to uplift and inspire. Maybe it was watching the president respond that drove Sousa to become the greatest composer of his time.

Yet young John Philip was not the only young person who listened to the Marine Band. Scores of other children had fathers who played in the group as well. These kids were given the same opportunity as was John Philip, so obviously being surrounded by music does not necessarily make someone a great musician. Besides environment, it takes a lot of innate talent and a real drive to make a mark in the musical universe. John Philip had both of these things too.

By the age of six, Sousa was playing the violin, piano, flute, cornet, baritone, trombone, and alto horn, as well as taking voice lessons. He quickly outgrew his teachers, and soon the student was doing the instructing. His talents were so great that at the tender age of thirteen the Marine Band waived its rules and allowed the young boy to join the organization. So John Philip became one of "the few, the proud, the brave, the marines," where he would remain until he was twenty-one. During this span he would not only be recognized as one of the unit's best musicians, but he would begin to compose music that the band would play. It is little wonder that the boy wonder was the pride of the orchestra known as "the President's Own."

In 1875, Sousa left the marines to perform with theater orchestras as a violinist. As a civilian, he would quickly rise to become the conductor of some of the most important groups in the country. He even arrived on Broadway just in time to conduct the debut of Gilbert & Sullivan's *H.M.S. Pinafore*. Now married, Sousa seemed ready to take the commercial music world by storm, but an unexpected event changed his course and, in the process, dramatically altered the course of American music.

In 1880, the Marine Band asked Sousa to again put on his uniform to lead the band in which he had once played. Not one to refuse a call to service, Sousa assumed direction of the famed ensemble just weeks after he had been asked. Under his leadership, the Marine Band would become the most important musical orchestra in the United States and one of the best in the entire world. Six years later, when he wrote "The Gladiator," Sousa was also recognized not just as an outstanding musician and the nation's best bandmaster, but as a top-notch composer. In 1888, when he penned "Semper Fidelis," the song that would become the official march standard of the United States Marine Corps, his status as one of the most popular forces in contemporary music was sealed.

Sousa was now a national icon; his popularity ranked with the president's. He was so well known that even in the days when newspapers and magazines devoted little space to photographs, he was recognized everywhere he went. His dinners and meetings were often interrupted by fans seeking his autograph. Musicians and composers from all over the world sought his advice. Businessmen often begged him to compose jingles for their company bands, and schoolchildren wrote him letters wanting to know how hard they would have to work to someday play in his orchestra. Though he was approaching middle age, he was the "rock" hero of his day.

In 1889, Frank Hatton, the editor of the *Washington Post*, contacted Sousa and requested an appointment. The two set up a meeting, where Hatton asked the conductor for a favor. The newspaper had put together an essay contest aimed at local schoolchildren. As Sousa was an idol to young and old alike, and as many of the area kids were fans of his music, Hatton wanted the conductor to compose something for the award presentation and debut it during the event where the winners would be announced. As both a friend of the newspaperman and someone deeply committed to education, Sousa agreed to work something up.

Hatton used the marine bandmaster's association with the contest to build interest in the competition as well as circulation for his newspaper. As Hatton's publicity campaign centering around Sousa generated record numbers of essay entries and scores of new subscribers, the conductor went to work writing a new song. As it turned out, the "March King," as he was now known throughout America and Europe, was not moved to compose a march. Sousa had recently developed a deep appreciation for a new dance called the two-step. He decided to write his new piece to fit the new dance craze.

No one now seems to remember who won the 1889 *Post*'s Amateur Authors Association top honors, but the song that the Marine Band played in honor of those winners will probably never be forgotten. As thousands looked on, Sousa conducted a number that left the audience stunned. He might have thought he had written a dance song, but all who heard its debut agreed that "The Washington Post" really was one of the most majestic march tunes that had ever been played. Even the Marine Band, which was used to the conductor's original music, couldn't wait to play it again.

"The Washington Post" received such a tremendous initial response that Sousa not only released the sheet music, but went into the studio and recorded the new song. Those with Edison phonograph machines quickly made the song the most popular release of the year in both the United States and Europe. Long before Chubby Checker got the world to twist, in every corner of the globe, men, women, and children were dancing the two-step to Sousa's "The Washington Post." This marked the first time that a popular American dance had created such a worldwide stir.

When Sousa left the Marine Corps to form his own band, he cut a new version of "The Washington Post." This time its sales were not driven by a popular dance; it simply stood on its own as a march tune. In 1895, the Columbia Records single ruled the national charts for the entire month of August. Along with "The Stars and Stripes Forever," this number would become one of the most popular songs written by the great American composer.

Today few people associate "The Washington Post March" with the newspaper. Yet the publicity that was generated by that initial connection in the late nineteenth century might well have guaranteed the success of the *Post*. While scores of other Washington dailies went under, it rose to the top. Today only a handful know that the song that now stirs the hearts of patriotic Americans on every occasion it is played really had its birth as a teacher's aid that encouraged participation in a writing contest.

29

WHEN JOHNNY COMES
MARCHING HOME

*f*or the man who is often called the "Father of the
American Band," life began not in the United
States, but across the Atlantic on Christmas Day,
1829, in Ballygar, county Galway, Ireland.

From an early age, Patrick Sarsfield Gilmore was constantly told that he was destined to be a priest. The priesthood was his parents' greatest dream, and they had practically
promised him to the church from the day he had been born.
His early education and his religious indoctrination pushed
him in a clerical direction. Gilmore might have ended up
wearing a white collar and dark coat if his father had not
taken him to a huge anti-British protest rally in the city of
Athlone. It was an exciting day full of fiery speeches and dec-
larations of independence. Yet all this was quickly forgotten
when the young boy suddenly heard music. From the
moment he first spied it, Gilmore's eyes did not once leave
the Ballygar Fife and Drum Band as the group marched

through the city. The music might not have quieted the crowd, but it left Gilmore awestruck. He pushed aside his parents' dreams of the priesthood and embraced a personal goal of joining the Ballygar Fife and Drum Corps. From that day forth, music was his life.

Gilmore first lived his dream in a small way when he became a member of a local band in Athlone. Yet being a part of this musical group was not enough. He studied music, learned to play the trumpet, and began to write songs. Gilmore was simply too talented for the small town, and he quickly grew beyond his teachers' abilities. In 1848, feeling a need to expand his knowledge and experience, he decided to further his musical training across the Atlantic. He initially landed in Canada, but within a few months he moved south and quickly became the head of the Boston Brigade Band.

During this period, Boston was an American cultural center. While there were many talented musicians in the city, few could hold a candle to Gilmore. His reputation quickly grew as a bandmaster and a trumpet player. He was lionized by both other musicians and the public. He could have stayed in Boston and always had a guaranteed place in the spotlight, yet it would be in the Protestant stronghold of Salem that the Irish Catholic would become a real star. Even in Salem, where he was initially viewed with great suspicion owing to his Catholic faith, Gilmore would soon win over the old American city with his trumpet and his vibrant personality.

By the mid-1850s, the trumpet player put together his own orchestra. Gilmore's Band, which featured the then radical concept of using two woodwinds for each brass instrument—a practice that is still employed today—quickly surfaced as New England's most famous ensemble. In 1855, Gilmore's Band also played at America's

When Johnny comes marching
   home again,
Hurrah! Hurrah!
We'll give him a hearty welcome
   then
Hurrah! Hurrah!
The men will cheer and the boys
   will shout
The ladies they will all turn out
And we'll all feel gay,
When Johnny comes marching
   home.

The old church bell will peal with
   joy
Hurrah! Hurrah!
To welcome home our darling boy

Hurrah! Hurrah!
The village lads and lassies say
With roses they will strew the way,
And we'll all feel gay
When Johnny comes marching
   home.

Get ready for the Jubilee,
Hurrah! Hurrah!
We'll give the hero three times
   three,
Hurrah! Hurrah!
The laurel wreath is ready now
To place upon his loyal brow
And we'll all feel gay
When Johnny comes marching
   home.

First Promenade Concert in Boston. That concert series continues today as the legendary Boston Pops.

Though Gilmore had been in the country for just over a decade, he was a staunch Union man. When the Civil War tore the Union apart in 1861, Gilmore's band played at pro–Union government rallies and military marches. Yet for the musician, simply playing old songs was not enough. He felt a need to write new music in order to further aid the cause of his adopted country.

Gilmore first realized his goal to bring his feelings of war and love of country to his music when he was performing for the Twelfth Massachusetts Regiment in Boston Harbor. During his stay, Gilmore heard a lone trooper singing "John Brown's Body." The bandmaster rewrote the music, arranged it for a band, and played it at every concert thereafter. Within months, thanks in large part to Gilmore's Band, "John Brown's Body" had become one of the best-known songs in the North. Julia Ward Howe heard the Gilmore tune in Washington and rewrote the lyrics. Howe's "Battle Hymn of the Republic" would become the Civil War's most remembered song. Though Gilmore's association with patriotic music would quickly be forgotten this time, he would soon write another song that would become almost as well known and have just as long a life as Ward's.

The Battle of Gettysburg would bring the horrors of war to almost every home in the United States. The death toll was so high that it seemed everyone knew someone who had died on those Pennsylvania fields. Though few realized it then, after Gettysburg the Confederate States would never again threaten the North. It would take another two years of fierce fighting, but the Union would be preserved. Yet at the moment when news reached Boston, thoughts were not as much focused on victory as they were on the great loss of life that had been realized during the battle.

With sad thoughts of weary men limping back to their loved ones, the musician hardly sensed any of the triumph and joy that should have come with victory. When a nation is torn by battle and infighting, Gilmore realized, winning would not bring great jubilation for those who had paid the price on the battlefield. He also knew that if he was depressed by just considering the toll of war, then millions of others would be as well. The bandmaster decided he would have to compose a song that would help change this gloomy attitude.

Gilmore knew of a song, "Johnny I Hardly Knew Ye," that had a stirring melody but a message that was anything but positive. In these lyrics war had taken a price that was almost too horrifying to consider. Gilmore realized that while this song fit the real national mood, it was not one that most wanted to hear.

While goin' the road to sweet Athy, hurroo, hurroo
While goin' the road to sweet Athy, hurroo, hurroo
While goin' the road to sweet Athy
A stick in me hand and a drop in me eye
A doleful damsel I heard cry,
Johnny I hardly knew ye.

With your drums and guns and drums and guns, hurroo, hurroo
With your drums and guns and drums and guns, hurroo, hurroo
With your drums and guns and drums and guns
The enemy nearly slew ye
Oh my darling dear, Ye look so queer
Johnny I hardly knew ye.

Where are your eyes that were so mild, hurroo, hurroo
Where are your eyes that were so mild, hurroo, hurroo
Where are your eyes that were so mild
When my heart you so beguiled
Why did ye run from me and the child
Oh Johnny, I hardly knew ye.

Where are your legs that used to run, hurroo, hurroo
Where are your legs that used to run, hurroo, hurroo
Where are your legs that used to run
When you went for to carry a gun
Indeed your dancing days are done
Oh Johnny, I hardly knew ye.

I'm happy for to see ye home, hurroo, hurroo
I'm happy for to see ye home, hurroo, hurroo
I'm happy for to see ye home
All from the island of Sulloon
So low in flesh, so high in bone
Oh Johnny, I hardly knew ye.

Ye haven't an arm, ye haven't a leg, hurroo, hurroo
Ye haven't an arm, ye haven't a leg, hurroo, hurroo
Ye haven't an arm, ye haven't a leg
Ye're an armless, boneless, chickenless egg
Ye'll have to put with a bowl out to beg
Oh Johnny, I hardly knew ye.

They're rolling out the guns again, hurroo, hurroo
They're rolling out the guns again, hurroo, hurroo
They're rolling out the guns again
But they never will take our sons again
No they never will take our sons again
Johnny I'm swearing to ye.

Gilmore believed that he could easily rearrange the tune to "Johnny," but for the song to inspire and uplift Americans, he knew he would have to compose new lyrics. The bandmaster pictured a heroic Johnny, one who was clear-eyed, strong, and confident. He coupled this image with those of the huge crowds and long parades that he believed would turn out to greet the veterans when they marched back to their home. With this in mind, Gilmore composed a song that turned his thoughts into music. Once it was completed, he immediately began to play it at Gilmore's Band concerts. Though there were hundreds of songs released with a war theme during the Civil War, Gilmore's stood out. It was easy to sing, evoked a message of glory, and made heroes out of the men who had so bravely fought to preserve the Union.

The sheet music for "When Johnny Comes Marching Home" was published in 1864 and quickly swept across the country. It was said to be one of Abraham Lincoln's favorites. He and many others felt that it created the climate needed to welcome back the millions who had experienced unspeakable horrors on the battlefields into a civilian life that offered hope and peace. It quickly became more than a song; it became the way America greeted its veterans.

Now known as "America's greatest bandleader," thanks in large part to "Johnny," by war's end Gilmore was an American superstar. The president even asked the bandmaster to lead a victory and peace celebration in New Orleans. Gilmore combined five hundred musicians with five thousand children in Lafayette Square. Southerners and Northerners came together once again to sing American patriotic music. Naturally, along with "The Star-Spangled Banner," Gilmore's "When Johnny Comes Marching Home" was one of the crowd's favorite. To the thousands who heard the chorus sing it that day, "Johnny" was inspirational, as well as a part of the healing process that Lincoln envisioned for the nation.

Over the course of his career Gilmore would direct a two-thousand-piece orchestra and a twenty-thousand-voice choir, and would be named music director for the centennial celebration in Philadelphia and the bandmaster in charge of the dedication of the Statue of Liberty in 1886. He would also make some of the first commercial recordings for Thomas Edison, initiate the now familiar tradition of greeting the New Year in Times Square, New York, and write hundreds of songs. Yet it is for "When Johnny Comes Marching Home" that he is now remembered.

Gilmore, perhaps the greatest bandmaster of all time, is now all but forgotten, except for a song meant to inspire those returning from a brutal war. And his simple song continues to inspire soldiers and their families.

30

YANKEE DOODLE

O f all America's patriotic songs, none is as nonsensical as "Yankee Doodle." Modern music historians would call this little ditty a novelty number. What began as an English number poking fun at New World colonists, "Yankee Doodle" became a Revolutionary War victory march that ultimately gave citizens of the United States a universal nickname. It is thanks to this song that in Europe, Asia, Africa, Australia, and just about everywhere else Americans are known simply as Yanks.

The tune and the humorous sentiment that are found in "Yankee Doodle" can be traced to England during the time of Oliver Cromwell in the 1600s. At that time the song, which was also familiar in other European locales, was called "Nancy Dawson." Soon, thanks to a division between very reform-minded religious groups and the establishment, "Nancy Dawson" became "Nankey Doodle."

The English upper crust sang "Nankey Doodle" at the expense of the Puritans. During the time of Charles I, the

Puritans did everything they could to separate themselves from all other British people. They spoke, dressed, and acted very differently. Many of them wore very short hair and were called Roundheads by Royalists, who wore their hair in long ringlets. As it was already common to ridicule the very proper and uncolorful Puritans in stories, the transition to ridiculing the group in music was a natural one.

Nankey Doodle came to town
Riding on a pony
Stuck a feather in his hat
upon a macaroni.

In the chorus, "Nankey" was a common term of contempt for the Puritans, who were viewed as being very simpleminded. The word "doodle" was defined in old English dictionaries as being one who was not very smart or sophisticated. As most in the British aristocracy felt there was nothing as dull or dimwitted as a Puritan, they used two words with the same meaning to provide the double insult found in "Nankey Doodle."

Macaroni might be something served with cheese now, but in seventeenth-century English it was a knot on a hat on which a feather was fastened. Seeing a Puritan wearing anything colorful, including a simple feather, would have been unheard of. So the English used the last line of the chorus to make a fashion statement on a group that distanced itself from anything that would have been considered representing London's latest styles.

Though often accompanied by laughter, the image that the song created was little more than a musical caricature. The message was laced with cruelty, and the song was often used in an attempt to con-

(THESE LYRICS ARE
FROM SHEET MUSIC
PUBLISHED IN 1799)
Father and I went down to camp,
Along with Captain Gooding,
There we see the men and boys,
As thick as hasty pudding.

Chorus:
Yankee doodle, keep it up,
Yankee doodle, dandy;
Mind the music and the step,
And with the girls be handy.

And there we see a thousand men,
As rich as "Squire David";
And what they wasted every day,
I wish it could be saved.

Chorus

The lasses they eat every day,
Would keep an house a winter;
They have as much that I'll be bound
They eat it when they're amind to.

Chorus

And there we see a swamping gun,
Large as a log of maple,
Upon a deuced little cart,
A load for father's cattle.

Chorus

And every time they shoot it off,
It takes a horn of powder;
It makes a noise like father's gun,
Only a nation louder.

Chorus

I went as nigh to one myself,
As 'Siah's underpining;
And father went as nigh again,
I thought the deuce was in him.

Chorus

Cousin Simon grew so bold,
I thought he would have cock'd it;
It scar'd me so, I shrink'd it off,
And hung by father's pocket.

Chorus

And Captain Davis had a gun,
He kind of clap'd his on't,
And struck a crooked stabbing iron
Upon the little end on't.

Chorus

And there I see a pumpkin shell
As big a mother's bason,

And every time they touch'd it off,
They scamper'd like the nation.

Chorus

I see a little barrel too,
The heads were made of leather,
They knock'd upon't with little
    clubs,
And call'd the folks together.

Chorus

And there was Captain Washington,
And gentlefolks about him,
They say he's grown so tarnal proud,
He will not ride without 'em.

Chorus

He got him on his meeting clothes,
Upon a slapping stallion,
He set the world along in rows,
In hundred and in millions.

Chorus

The flaming ribbons in their hats,
They look'd so taring fine, ah,
I wanted pockily to get,
To give to my Jemimah.

Chorus

I see another snarl of men
A digging graves, they told me,
So tarnal long, so tarnal deep,
They 'tended they should hold me.

Chorus

It scar'd me so, I hook'd it off,
Nor stopt, as I remember,
Nor turn'd about till I got home,
Lock'd up in mother's chamber.

Chorus

vince young Puritans to leave the movement. To escape this type of persecution, many Puritans eventually decided to leave their native country and try starting over in the New World. Little did they know that the British ridicule and the song they so despised would follow them to Plymouth Rock and beyond.

It is said that the first Native Americans that met the Puritans could not pronounce the word "English." For some reason when the Massachusetts Indians said "English" it came out "Yankee." British soldiers and other government officials heard the Indians use this term when trading with the Puritans and began to refer to these religious Pilgrims as Yankees rather than Nankeys. While the word might have changed, the meaning remained the same well into the next century.

In 1713, a farmer named Jonathon Hastings lived just off the Harvard campus in Cambridge, Massachusetts. He was not a Puritan, but as he was a bit dimwitted and slow in both movement and speech, he fit the stereotype invented by the English. Hastings would often sell what he raised to the college. He was fond of telling those with whom he negotiated that they were getting a "Yankee good horse" or a "Yankee good deal." Usually, the person receiving the goods got the short end of the stick. Long after the farmer died, students at Harvard still called anyone who tried to make trades on goods or services a Yankee Jonathon, and the person who was taken by one of the traders was often laughed at because he had been "yanked" around. Then the old Puritan song was revived and sung to further emphasize just how stupid the trade had been.

Even though it was somewhat popular at Harvard, "Yankee Doodle" would probably have been forgotten, as were most of the silly songs of the time, if a British doctor had not decided to rewrite it to poke fun at a group of farmers who had volunteered to fight with the English in the French and Indian War.

In 1755, the extremely proud British regulars who had come to American shores to fight the hated French wore carefully tailored uniforms. Each trooper was outfitted in the very same way. As they marched across the colonies, their red coats and spit-shined boots looked incredible. To make sure that the soldiers kept their regulation look in perfect order, the British officers held numerous inspections. It was said that even when the English army lost, they looked good doing it.

The colonists who formed the militia that joined the British troops looked much different from their English counterparts. The Americans were dressed in whatever they could find. These part-time soldiers were at best ragtag, shoddy, unkempt, and dirty. Outfitted in a rainbow of colors, they were a laughingstock in the eyes of the Englishmen.

A British doctor assigned to the redcoats, Richard Shackburg, decided to rewrite the old "Nankey Doodle" into a ditty that addressed all of the shortcomings of the American troopers. Shackburg taught his version of "Yankee Doodle" to the English regulars. Armed with this verbal ammunition, the spit-shined chorus were ready when the colonists marched in to join them. As one voice the English soldiers serenaded the Americans with the new version of the old song. The Americans continued to hear the song almost every day for the entire span of the war.

And two decades later, when the British returned to American shores to stifle the colonists' revolution, they were so confident that they again used "Yankee Doodle" as a weapon of ridicule against soldiers and civilians alike. Yet in a strange twist of fate, the man who led Americans during the Revolution would transform "Yankee Doodle" into a source of colonial pride.

When the Americans finally defeated England and sent them and their fancy uniforms back to the mother country, the British commander, Lord Cornwallis, had to pay a visit to General George

Washington. With his well-dressed troopers following behind him, Cornwallis paraded in front of thousands of Americans who looked at the fallen enemy's leader and his men with great disdain. As they approached the assigned meeting point where the British officer was to turn his sword over to the leader of the American rebellion, General Washington gave a signal. When Cornwallis eyed the victorious commander and his ragtag troops, the American band began playing "Yankee Doodle." This was Washington's way of asking which side was the simpleminded one now. Because of this, throughout the new United States, Americans celebrated their freedom by singing the song they had once scorned.

During every American war that followed the fight for independence, "Yankee Doodle" has been played with pride. The song was again used as a victory march in the Civil War, American men were greeted by this number when they arrived in Europe during World War I, and a new generation of GIs heard "Yankee Doodle" sung by happy Frenchmen during World War II. Even in Korea and Vietnam, refugee children serenaded U.S. soldiers with the old song.

Today, to most Americans, a Yankee might well be a member of the famed New York baseball team, but throughout the rest of the world a Yankee is anyone who comes from the United States.

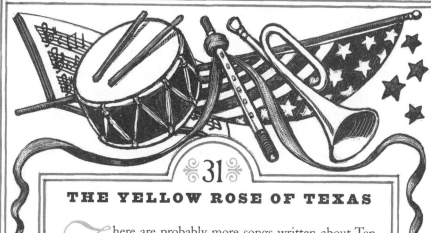

31

THE YELLOW ROSE OF TEXAS

There are probably more songs written about Tennessee and Texas than any other states in the Union. For some reason there is a romance associated with these places that has long inspired songwriters. Though it wasn't the first popular American waltz, the "Tennessee Waltz" became the most loved. Every other state plays second fiddle when it comes to waltzes and Tennessee. But Texas has an even larger lock on inspired song concepts.

Surely the central portion of scores of states is known as the "heart," but who could imagine a song entitled "Deep in the Heart of Illinois" taking the nation by storm? Maybe the "eyes" of Vermont are on you, but who cares? But the list of Texas-defined musical titles goes on and on. Yet of all the Lone Star songs, there is one that really stands out. Written in the days just before the Texas Revolution, "The Yellow Rose of Texas" quickly became one of America's best-loved folk songs, and it has stood the test of time by topping popular music charts more than 120 years after it was written. It was one of the nation's favorite songs during the Civil War, and American soldiers took it with them to every corner of the globe in the international wars that littered the world in the twentieth century. It was also one of the first widely popular American songs written by an African American.

"The Yellow Rose of Texas" was initially published in New York City in 1853. The copyright stated that the song had been composed by a man whose initials were J.K. The publisher's claim that J.K. wanted to remain anonymous was probably nothing more than a ruse for stealing the publishing rights. This was a common publishing practice with folk songs up until World War II. Whoever registered songs owned all rights, and the people who wrote them were quickly forgotten.

J.K., or whatever his initials really were, was probably a runaway or former slave who had arrived in Texas during the early 1830s. As slavery was frowned upon by the Mexican government, a black man had a better chance of making a life for himself in Lone Star land than he did even in most of the northern states. Yet this window of opportunity would be short-lived. When Texas won the war for independence, slavery was reinstated. Since his identity remains unknown, what happened to him after the war is a mystery. All that is left of J.K.'s story is his song.

The earliest surviving transcript of "The Yellow Rose of Texas" is currently on display in Austin. The notes on this piece of linen paper give strong credence to the fact that the song's writer was an African American from Tennessee. As many of the song's words were incorrectly spelled, it seems clear that the composer also lacked much formal education. Still, if J.K. had been a slave, he had probably been a household servant, as field hands rarely learned how to read or write.

ORIGINAL LYRICS

There's a yellow rose in Texas, that
  I am going to see,
No other darky knows her, no
  darky only me
She cryed so when I left her it like
  to broke my heart,
And if I ever find her, we never-
  more will part.

Chorus:
She's the sweetest rose of color this
  darky ever knew,
Her eyes are bright as diamonds,
  they sparkle like the dew;
You may talk about your Dearest
  May, and sing of Rosa Lee,
But the Yellow Rose of Texas beats
  the belles of Tennessee.

Chorus

When the Rio Grande is flowing,
  the starry skies are bright,
She walks along the river in the
  quiet summer night:
She thinks if I remember, when we
  parted long ago,
I promised to come back again, and
  not to leave her so.

Chorus

Oh now I'm going to find her, for
  my heart is full of woe,
And we'll sing the songs together,
  that we sung so long ago.
We'll play the banjo gaily, and we'll
  sing the songs of yore,
And the Yellow Rose of Texas
  shall be mine forevermore.

If the song's writer was a former slave from Tennessee, then who was his rose and why was she yellow rather than red or pink? The answer can be found in the language of the times. In the early nineteenth century, mulatto men and women were almost always referred to as yellow, and Rose was a common pet name for a woman in the South.

The most famous mulatto in all of colonial Texas was an indentured servant named Emily West. Emily was an attractive woman of mixed ancestory who had once lived in New York. She was probably brought to Texas by entrepreneur James Morgan around 1835. Morgan, a Philadelphian, was investing New Yorkers' money in businesses and land in Texas. Morgan needed cheap labor to build his ranches, docks, and stores, and as slavery was illegal in this part of what was then Mexico, with a simple stroke of a pen he made his slaves indentured servants. To assure that these men and women would continue to *serve* him for a long time, the period of indenturement was not the normal seven years, but rather ninety-nine.

Little is known of Emily West's background, but many believe she chose to join Ward in order to escape a harsh life in New York. She was probably around twenty, possibly a native of the Caribbean, and the few records that exist indicate that her beauty was rivaled only by her intelligence. As soon as she arrived in Texas, she adopted the last name of Morgan and became an important part of her master's business operation.

When war broke out the next year, Morgan's small settlement had great strategic importance to the Texas rebels as the primary shipping point for goods coming to supply Sam Houston's troops.

Tradition has it that on April 18, 1836, as General Santa Anna positioned his army to attack the Texas rebels, he spotted Emily

West. Rather than moving ahead against the Texans, Santa Anna had his men capture the mulatto and bring her to his tent. Intent on enjoying Emily's charms, he temporarily forgot about Sam Houston and his band of rebels. Supposedly Emily played along only to halt the Mexican advance.

Setting up camp along the river in a spot that would be hard to defend, the lustful Santa Anna got to know Emily better. As he did, the Texas forces silently approached. The general was still with his "Yellow Rose" when Houston attacked the next day. Santa Anna and his army were caught completely by surprise. It was reported that the general escaped capture by running from the scene clothed only in a nightshirt.

There are some who speculate that rather than occupying Santa Anna for the glory of Texas, Emily West was simply trying to align herself with someone who had more money and power than did her current master. For her efforts at the Battle of San Jacinto, Emily was immediately made a Texas hero. Morgan reportedly freed her and paid for her trip back to New York. What became of this woman when she returned to the East Coast is unknown.

Emily West was beautiful, was well known by black, brown, and white men in Texas, and was an important historical figure. Most early manuscripts of "The Yellow Rose of Texas" were transcribed with another title, "Emily, the Maid of Morgan's Point." Unless this title was added as an after-the-fact salute to Emily West, it would seem that she really was Texas's "Yellow Rose."

Men and women traveling to and from Texas took the folk song east. By the time it was published, it was well known throughout America. By the beginning of the Civil War, "The Yellow Rose of

Texas" was even popular in Europe, having become a favorite with traveling minstrel groups and Gypsy bands. Yet even as the world was learning the original words of this Negro folk song, it was being rewritten.

Soldiers of the Confederacy often sang around the campfires and as they marched. Along with "Dixie," their favorite standard was "The Yellow Rose of Texas." Yet a song written by a former slave about a mixed-race sweetheart didn't go well with "the Southern cause." Therefore, the words were changed. "Darky" became "soldier," and other references to race were removed. Then, in 1864, when it was obvious that the war was over, a fourth verse was added that reflected men beaten and bloodied while fighting a hopeless war.

She's the sweetest rose of color this soldier ever knew,
Her eyes are bright as diamonds, they sparkle like the dew;
You may talk about your Dearest May, and sing of Rosa Lee,
But the Yellow Rose of Texas beats the belles of Tennessee.

Chorus:
When the Rio Grande is flowing, the starry skies are bright,
She walks along the river in the quiet summer night:
She thinks if I remember, when we parted long ago,
I promised to come back again, and not to leave her so.

Oh now I'm going to find her, for my heart is full of woe,
And we'll sing the songs together, that we sung so long ago
We'll play the banjo gaily, and we'll sing the songs of yore,
And the Yellow Rose of Texas shall be mine forevermore. [Chorus]

And now I'm going southward, for my heart is full of woe,
I'm going back to Georgia, to see my Uncle Joe.
You may talk about your Beauregard, and sing of Bobbie Lee,
But the gallant Hood of Texas played hell in Tennessee. [Chorus]

"The Yellow Rose of Texas" remained a favorite folk song long after the end of the Civil War. No longer just a Southern standard, it became the folk song that signified the expansion of America to the west. It was taught in public schools from coast to coast, was used by dance bands and orchestras, and was even written into Broadway musicals. During both World War I and World War II, American troops sang the song on the battle lines and marched to "Yellow Rose" in boot camps. Yet it would take a New York–born bandleader to turn "The Yellow Rose of Texas" into a national sensation and cement it as a song that is played at many patriotic celebrations to this day.

In the forties, Mitch Miller worked with some of the greatest recording stars in the entertainment industry. An orchestra leader and arranger, Mitch also hit upon a surefire formula for selling his own records. He recorded albums for music lovers to sing along with while they listened at home. This "Sing Along with Mitch" concept really began to gel in the mid-fifties. Printing the lyrics on the albums' back covers, Mitch sold hundreds of thousands of records to people who just wanted to add their voices to the backup strains of an orchestra and chorus. While Miller had some initial success using this formula, his idea wouldn't really strike gold until he found the perfect sing-along tune.

When the bandleader recorded "The Yellow Rose of Texas," he cut a number whose lyrics were familiar to most Americans and that was easy to sing. "Yellow Rose" became an instant hit. Released as a single in the summer of 1955, it would knock Bill Haley and His Comets' "Rock Around the Clock" out of *Billboard*'s top spot on September 6. "The Yellow Rose of Texas" would stay number 1 for six weeks.

The lyrics that fueled Miller's long chart-topping single were a bit different from either the original or the Civil War version of "Yellow Rose." Today, these words remain the best known.

A beautiful mulatto woman, a man who had known slavery first-hand—the odds of these two individuals meeting in Texas in the days leading up to the most important battle in Lone Star history were indeed long. There is irony that the song's writer and subject would play a part in a victory that established slavery in a nation they fought to free. While we will never know if the writer and the Rose got back together, many Americans can say with great conviction that "you may talk about your Clementine and sing of Rosalee, but 'The Yellow Rose of Texas' is the only *song* for me."

32

YOU'RE A GRAND OLD FLAG

ame had come early and easily to George M. Cohan. In 1900, he was emerging as the star of a family traveling music ensemble known as the Four Cohans. Literally having been born into the business, on stage by the time he was walking, he was a theater natural. Even though he received no formal education, by his teens Cohan was writing and selling songs, organizing shows, and working with newspapers on publicity. At twenty, Cohan moved to center stage—he was not just the star of the show, but he had replaced his father as manager as well. With George in command, the Four Cohans were playing the best theaters from coast to coast and commanding as much as one thousand dollars per week. This was an astounding sum considering that most common laborers made less than a dollar a day.

Cohan, who rubbed many people the wrong way, often pointed to his Irish heritage as the reason he was opinionated, brash, and arrogant. Yet most thought it was just George being George. He knew he was talented and spent a portion of every day selling that fact to others. It was probably his salesmanship and talent working in tandem that helped make the Cohan family headliners. Yet even though things were running smoothly and continued success seemed assured, George sensed that times were changing and the act had to as well. With this in mind he began to look and work toward the time when he would be the whole show.

In 1901, Cohan wrote and starred in his first real musical play, *The Governor's Son*. It failed at the Broadway box office. Two years later he penned another full-length musical, *Running for Office*. Again his politically inspired effort failed to draw a crowd. Cohan would probably have been forced back on the road if he hadn't teamed with businessman Sam Harris. Cohan and Harris combined talent with pragmatism and ended up with the Broadway hit *Little Johnny Jones*.

In 1905, George M. Cohan was on top of the world, riding the success of *Little Johnny Jones* and its two hit songs, "Give My Regards to Broadway" and "Yankee Doodle Dandy." Even though the singer-writer was quickly becoming one of the hottest commodities on the New York stage, Cohan realized that while he might have a major hit under his belt, a performer was only as good as his latest play. For his follow-up he found his inspiration in a very unexpected place, lifted from the words of a very unusual man.

Cohan's first Broadway success allowed him to give up horse-drawn carriages and become a part of the motoring generation. Over the remainder of his life, his love of cars would lead to his owning scores of them in every color and style. He was riding in one of his first automobiles one day when he spotted an elderly man walking along the road. The star ordered his driver to stop. Cohan then asked if the man would like a ride.

Cohan realized that the man was obviously not well-to-do. He also figured that this was probably the first time the old gentleman had ever been given the opportunity to ride in a car. Though neither man considered it at that moment, this was really a unique meeting of generations, a person from a past period of rural American pioneering and the young, energetic writer who couldn't wait to see what tomorrow had to offer.

Cohan was used to being the center of attention on stage and off and usually dominated every conversation. Yet this time the songsmith listened rather than talked. What he heard would not just affect his own life by inspiring his second Broadway hit, but would bring something very special to the fabric of American life as well.

Cohan, seemingly fascinated by his guest, studied him carefully. He looked just like another grandfather type except for one peculiar quirk. As he rode down the highway, the gray-headed man, his body bent, his skin wrinkled, held a tattered old piece of multicolored cloth in his hands. The man's hand never stopped moving, continually stroking the rag as if it were a favorite pet. After a while, as he grew used to watching the world race by at almost ten miles an hour, the old man began to talk. Over the next few minutes Cohan was only mildly surprised to discover that his guest had fought in the Civil War. The man was proud of that fact too. His stories clearly showed that he clung to his past in the Grand Army of the Republic like a child clutches a favorite toy. In a voice weakened by time, he told the "Toast of Broadway" many tales, including one that centered on the Battle of Gettysburg. That was the day that, as a much younger man, he had charged the Union forces against the South's famed General Pickett. The veteran then pridefully shared with Cohan that he had been the flag bearer. As others around him fell to the ground, injured or dead, as the banner he held high was shot by hundreds of rounds of lead balls, and as the battle slowly turned in the Union's favor, the young man was shaken to the core. How he had survived he didn't know. He heard scores of bullets fly past his head on several occasions. Yet to him surviving was not as important as was the fact he had never dropped the American flag. He had held the country's banner high throughout the entire battle.

As the old man finished his story, Cohan watched him continue gently to pat the carefully folded, ragged piece of cloth that sat in his lap. "It was all for this," the old vet sighed. "She's a grand old rag, Mr. Cohan. Yes, she's a grand old rag." It was only then that the songwriter realized that the cloth the man held so carefully was not just a piece of material from an old shirt or coat but the flag that he had carried but never dropped during the battle against Pickett's men.

Cohan had always, and in the future always would, write his plays before he composed the music to put with his stories. Yet the image of the man in the car would not leave him alone, thus forcing him to reverse his normal creative process. Within hours of having stopped to offer the old man a ride, the composer scribbled down his initial concept—a number based on the old man's experience and his genuine love of country. Once he had finished the song, Cohan went to work writing a play that could frame and spotlight this new composition. The resulting musical was named after a fictitious relative of the "Father of the Country."

George Washington Jr. was not just another Cohan comedy; it was in fact a whodunit musical comedy. This minor detective yarn also managed to do what George knew best, embrace patriotism and the American Dream. Best of all, it was very funny. At one point one of the characters tells the story about George Washington tossing a silver dollar across the Potomac River. When another character comments that the river was very wide and that it would seem to have been impossible for even the great general to throw a dollar that far, the first character replies, "A dollar went a lot further then." Cohan's vaudeville background served this project well, as jokes like that continued throughout the whole play.

Yet the highlight of this musical was not the humor or the whodunit plot; it was the moment when an actor costumed as a Civil War veteran handed Cohan a tattered battle flag. As everyone looked at the old banner, the old man said, "It's a grand old rag." Then, as if by magic, Cohan and company launched into the song that had inspired the play.

The audience was not just enthralled. Many were moved to tears, while others shouted and pumped their fists. It was obvious from the response that Cohan had a winning show on his hands, as well as a song that could follow "Give My Regards to Broadway" and "I'm a Yankee Doodle Dandy" on the hit-parade charts.

The next day several reviewers questioned Cohan's regard and respect for the American flag. One reporter wrote that Cohan had slandered the nation itself by calling the Stars and Stripes a "rag." Cohan immediately sensed that *George Washington Jr.* might well be booed off stage if "The Grand Old Rag" created a firestorm of controversy and called into question Cohan's own love of country. He had to act and act quickly.

That night the play continued, but this time Cohan replaced "rag" with "flag." This revision not only saved his play but made the song more widely appealing. Bill Murray rushed into the recording studio and cut a solo version of the newest Cohan song. His cut would hit number 1 in the nation in January 1906. Scores of other artists would also record "You're a Grand Old Flag." The Prince's Quartet and Arthur Pryor's Band hit the Top 10 as well. Within months, thanks to Victrola records and sheet-music sales, millions who had never heard of *George Washington Jr.* knew both the words and the music to "Grand Old Flag." Within a year of the opening of the musical it had inspired, the Cohan tune had become the most recorded and beloved patriotic ode in the country at that time.

Though "You're a Grand Old Flag" would have remained an important American standard without any help from history, World War I assured this tune's place as the country's most upbeat and uplifting patriotic song. Though it is neither maudlin nor deeply sentimental, along with "The Star-Spangled Banner," it is simply one of the most beloved songs in American history. This should hardly be surprising considering that it was inspired by a single man's courage and devotion to his country. Thanks to George M. Cohan, a Civil War flag bearer didn't carry his flag only on that day of the Battle at Gettysburg; his spirit is alive and carrying the Stars and Stripes even today.

ACKNOWLEDGMENTS

The author wishes to thank the following: John Hillman, Rheda Jones, Madeleine Morel, the United States Coast Guard, the United States Marine Corps, the United States Navy, the United States Air Force, the United States Army, Joan Leslie, Louise Mandrell, Peter Kiefer, Charlie Daniels, Paula Szeigis, the Hillsboro Public Library, Baylor University's Moody Library.